MAFIA QUEENS OF MUMBAI

S. Hussain Zaidi is one of India's finest crime writers. He is the author of several best-selling books, including *Black Friday, Dongri to Dubai* and *My Name Is Abu Salem*. He was Resident Editor of *The Asian Age* and also worked for *The Indian Express, Mid-Day* and *Mumbai Mirror* in a career spanning three decades. His books have been the inspiration for several movies, including *Black Friday, Gangubai Kathiawadi, Phantom, Shootout at Wadala* and *Class of '83*. Currently he is working on several non-fiction projects and writing scripts for Netflix and Amazon Prime.

Jane Borges is a senior journalist and editor. Her bylines have appeared in *Sunday Mid-Day, The Asian Age* and *Muscat Daily*. Her debut novel, *Bombay Balchão,* was shortlisted for the Sahitya Akademi Yuva Puruskar and Atta Galatta-Bangalore Literature Festival Book Prize. In 2022, she won the RedInk Journalism Award in the lifestyle and entertainment category. She lives in Mumbai.

Praise for *Mafia Queens of Mumbai*

'Thirteen true stories of black marketeers, prostitution ringleaders, and trained assassins hit these pages with a convincing splatter. They may call it trade paper, but this is pulpy at its gritty, graphic best, steeped in juicy detail and relishing every suspenseful wit ... The rare book that, like *Mafia Queens*, peels back Mumbai's thin veneer of civilization isn't merely sensational; it's essential to completing the portrait of a corrupt city.'

Mint

'Zaidi has managed to be both a reporter and a raconteur in his stories about the underworld. *Mafia Queens* has dollops of drama in its accounts of singular, fearless women.'

TimeOut Mumbai

'Without seeming to romanticise their exploits or turn them into poster girls of crime, Zaidi and Borges offer perceptive glimpses of the women's complex minds to show how they pushed the boundaries of dominant moral codes of their times.'

Deccan Herald

'... a valuable piece of reportage, for it offers new insights into a world for which people have endless fascination, and it does so through a unique perspective.'

Sunday Guardian

'*Mafia Queens*, by virtue of its very stark simplicity is a revelation, a rare treat for the discerning lover of crime stories. Intricately researched, told with restraint and reserve, the book explores a bold and original theme. And in doing so, completely remaps the city's gender geographies.'

The Hindu

'... what makes this book a compelling read is that it tells the stories of very real women of our generation.'

The Hindu Business Line

'... vibrates with drama, intrigue and unexpected pathos.'

Hindustan Times

'As gripping as its protagonists.'

Times of India

S. HUSSAIN ZAIDI
WITH JANE BORGES

MAFIA QUEENS OF MUMBAI

STORIES OF WOMEN FROM THE GANGLANDS

First published by Tranquebar, an imprint of westland ltd, in 2010

Published in hardback by Westland Books, a division of Nasadiya Technologies Private Limited, in 2023

Published in paperback in 2025

No. 269/2B, First Floor, 'Irai Arul', Vimalraj Street, Nethaji Nagar, Alapakkam Main Road, Maduravoyal, Chennai 600095

ISBN: 9789371971980

10 9 8 7 6 5 4 3 2

Typeset by SÜRYA, New Delhi

Printed at Thomson Press India Private Limited

For our beloved parents, Khatoon and Ashfaq Husain,
Sandra and Johnny Borges; the light of our lives

CONTENTS

FOREWORD

Crime is juicier than spirituality. Guns are more attractive than roses. And thus—at least to me—the stories about the lives of gangsters are much more fascinating to share than that of saints.

I felt that crime reporting in India is limited only to the columns of daily newspapers and the stories die shortly after they are published. It is truly rare that a book seeks to preserve such stories for posterity and specifically, for fans like me.

As a filmmaker, my need for such stories is even more so. I always felt handicapped and a tad frustrated, because there was no way I could dig into the lives or events in the glorious criminal past of the great city of dreams, once called Bombay and now known as Mumbai. But the time came when I had to change my opinion. It was when I saw the film *Black Friday* (made by my dear friend and a fantastic filmmaker, Anurag Kashyap), which is based on the book of the same title, authored by S. Hussain Zaidi. The book was a thoroughly researched account of the reasons and the conspiracy that led to the horrible 1993 Mumbai serial blasts and the repercussions that followed.

Hussain's was a name stuck forever in my mind after that. I found a ray of hope in his work. I decided to follow his crime stories and therefore, had to change my newspaper every time he switched jobs.

Finally I met him during the research work of my film *Kaminey*. He was of great help, of course, taking me to people and places in order for me to have a glance into the drug-trafficking business of the city, an inseparable part of the Mumbai mafia. It was then that I made him promise to give me the first right of refusal of his next work for a film adaptation.

Precisely two years later I got a call from him, asking me to write the foreword of the book that you have in your hand right now—*The Mafia Queens of Mumbai*. Stories that I and I'm sure most of you, have never heard.

Personally, I enjoy the female protagonist or antagonist much more than the male one. Lady Macbeth is more complex and fascinating a character than Macbeth or King Duncan. Madam Bovary, Anna Karenina, Phoolan Devi, Indira Gandhi and Sonia Gandhi are, to me, much more interesting than their male counterparts.

As expected, this read was a delightful journey; or rather should I say, a rollercoaster ride. Sometimes hilarious, sometimes full of sorrow, sometimes horrifying but always dramatic. The shrewd Jenabai Daaruwali who made notorious ganglords like Karim Lala, Haji Mastan and 'our own' Dawood Ibrahim dance to the movement of her fingers just like a conductor of a big philharmonic orchestra. The ironic tale of the queen of Kamathipura, Gangubai, fighting to get recognition for the existence and importance of sex workers in society. Or the melancholic tale of a wife looking for revenge for her slain husband from none other than Dawood Ibrahim ...

The writing is so visual that it makes you feel as if you are watching a movie, inter-cutting between various tracks. The stories are almost cinematically structured, flashing back or forward and taking one through numerous time passages. Honestly, it left me struggling to decide which one to choose to adapt to celluloid!

So I proudly welcome you into the world of these beautiful, kind and cunning warring queens who broke through the glass ceiling in the absolute stronghold of brutal masculinity called the Underworld.

Mumbai ki queen kaun? Turn the pages and make your choice.

VISHAL BHARDWAJ

INTRODUCTION

Mafia Queens of Mumbai is the translation of a decade-and-a-half-long dream. During the late Nineties, when crime reporting was still my bailiwick, I became fascinated with women criminals. I realised they were gutsier, far more scheming and lethal when it came to pursuing their goals.

One episode that left an indelible imprint on my mind was the story of Lallan Bhabhi. In the world of Bhais (criminals) she was the Bhabhi, one of the cogs in the petrol adulteration cartel. On a rainy evening, she was arrested and taken to the Sewree Police Station in south Mumbai. As per the norm, she was allowed to make one phone call. Generally, the accused uses the opportunity to inform their relatives about their arrest or hire a lawyer for bail proceedings.

This woman, sitting in the police station right under the cops' noses, called her house and instructed her younger brother, 'I am not coming home tonight, please shift the kitchen.'

The cop who narrated the story to me later said they were mystified by the whole conversation. 'Why would a woman who has just been arrested by the cops, be more concerned about her kitchen than her children, husband or her own release?'

The police knew it was futile to question her; she was hardly expected to be honest with the law. They could not use unconventional methods to make a woman talk, so they dispatched a police party to her house and asked her brother about the whole conversation. The boy immediately cracked and revealed that she meant the fresh stock of adulterated petrol which was not seized by the cops should be immediately shifted to some other hideout before the police learned of its existence.

Lallan Bhabhi showed her mettle to the cops; she was unfazed by the law. For her, being in police custody was just an interlude before resuming her criminal activities and she didn't want any financial loss despite her being incarcerated. She wanted to keep her petrol adulteration business thriving and running.

As a writer and journalist, it was a seminal moment for me. I was intrigued. I began compiling data and began taking a special interest in crimes where women figured prominently. It might come handy if I wrote a book, I told myself.

And after having written about all kinds of criminals over the years, I can say with firm conviction that when it comes to gender dynamics, it is much easier to be a

Dawood Ibrahim than a Jenabai Daaruwali. If you sift through the gangs of Chhotas (Rajan and Shakeel), you will find clones galore, but you will rarely come across a Sapna Didi, a woman who dared to stand up against Dawood and was given a dastardly death by the don's acolytes. Of the twenty-two stab wounds inflicted on her, four were specifically targeted at her private parts, a grisly message of warning to other women not to dally with the mafia.

This book is an attempt to understand the complex minds and the psyche of women criminals. It is in no way meant to glorify them. On the other hand, these women were not blank slates written upon by dangerous male mafia members. There is no simplistic cause-effect way of looking at their lives. There is no doubt that for these women, crime was not only a way of transcending their poverty and limitations but also a life-saving concept. By focusing on these women, I am not trying to essentialise the nature of female criminals. They are fascinating women because they pushed the boundaries of our dominant moral codes.

Compiling the extraordinary and powerful tales of thirteen women from the world of crime and the underworld was overwhelmingly challenging and arduous, especially because a number of them flourished at a time when crimes by women were barely documented or acknowledged. These include the stories of bootlegger Jenabai Daaruwali and brothel madam Gangubai Kathiawadi.

As journalists the first lesson we learnt was not to sit on judgment but raise questions. In the stories that you will read, we have desisted from being judgmental and have stuck to facts. We have relied heavily on court documents, police records, cop historians, reliable journalists and published news stories in major national dailies.

In the absence of these, we have interviewed relatives, neighbours, retired policemen, veteran journalists and other independent witnesses. We ensured that any account which seemed controversial was corroborated by two separate parties. Those accounts which seemed contradictory to each other were ignored.

This book is an attempt at accurate and true story-telling. It is not a piece of fiction. We have taken literary license only in those places where we feel it is absolutely necessary to add graphic drama to the story, but without any sort of dilution to the authenticity of the incidents.

ONE

THE WILY OLD WOMAN OF DONGRI

Chapter 1

AT THE GRAVEYARD

The Arabian Sea, murky and grey, flails and lashes against the giant tetra-pods on the Queen's Necklace near Marine Lines. The skies have opened up to let loose a welcome spell of rain after playing hide-and-seek with the city for days.

Not long ago, until the mid-Eighties, you could stand on the footboard of a Western local train and watch the shimmering sea as your train whizzed past Charni Road to Marine Lines. The name Marine Lines is a British legacy, a throwback to a time when the British put Mumbai on the trade route in the mid-nineteenth century by linking the city with an amazing network of railheads. Marine Lines comes from Marine Battalion Lines, a British military establishment. The battalion was later converted to an air force residence quarters, and you can still visit it just south of Metro Adlabs. If you get off at Marine Lines station, only a road—known as V. Thackersey Marg—separates the sea from the famous Marine Drive promenade.

Abutting the station is Bada Qabrastan, a sprawling 7.5 acres that is a reminder and a testimony to man's mortality. In fact, the cemetery—a hundred-and-fifty-years-old—is so close to the station that commuters cut across it before taking the stairs leading to the over-bridge at the north end of the station.

As I enter Bada Qabarstan, sheets of rain pelt the tombstones, adding to the gloom. It is for a story on Haji Mastan that I am here. It is his barsi, or death anniversary, and I was told that the yesteryear's don, who was Mumbai's most notorious gold smuggler, is remembered every year by his three daughters with a profusion of flowers and rose petals.

This is not an unheard of phenomenon in Mumbai; the rich like to remember their dead in various ways. There's an apocryphal story about Dawood Ibrahim's police constable father. Apparently when Ibrahim Kaskar passed away, his son Dawood arranged for truckloads of rose petals to be showered on his father's grave. For three days, they say, the fragrance of roses wafted across the graveyard.

Futilely trying to sidestep puddles, I walk along a neat, well-maintained line of graves. Haji Mastan's final resting place is easy to locate—the inscriptions are both in Urdu and English. Fresh rose petals have been laid out on the grave but the rumoured huge mounds of flowers are missing. I see a few people gathered around the grave, reciting from the Koran supplications. Perhaps I'd better confirm that this is, in fact, the don's grave. I gather courage and ask an attendant, 'Kya yeh Haji Mastan ki qabar hai?' (Is this Haji Mastan's grave?)

Some of the mourners give me disapproving looks but one of them nods. I look back at the grave and wonder why Mastan's daughters did not construct a more elaborate tombstone, a shrine-like edifice like several I can see around, instead of the simple, flat one they have chosen. How the mighty fall, I think, and decide to wander around.

This is my first visit to Bada Qabrastan. I am told that several of the men who ruled Mumbai's underbelly with an iron fist were laid to rest here—Karim Lala, Ibrahim Dada, Rahim Khan, Dawood Ibrahim's brother Sabir Kaskar, to name a few. Now that the Haji Mastan flower story doesn't seem to be working out, perhaps I could check the epitaphs on the graves of these dons.

I ask—perhaps a bit naively—'Kya yahan underworld walon ke liye alag section hain?' (Are the members of the underworld buried in a different corner of the graveyard?) One man in a chequered lungi, tied up so that it ends just over his knees, and a crumpled kurta, laughs. 'Miyan, the qabrastan is the real underworld; whoever comes here goes to the underworld. Yahan saare underworld ke raja aur rani aakar so jate hain.' (All the underworld kings and queens have to come rest here finally.)

'Underworld ki rani?' I wondered aloud. 'Do you mean the wives of the underworld dons?'

He looks around and then looks at me pointedly. I slip him a fifty-rupee note, which disappears into his baggy kurta.

'Mastan had a sister ... some woman called ... I can't remember her full name, she was some Gandhi. She tied a rakhi to our former prime minister Morarji Desai. Yashwantrao Chavan—who was chief minister of Maharashtra—used to respect her a lot also. She was the queen of the Mumbai underworld; no one like her will ever be seen again.'

Has the old man gone senile, I wonder. As a crime reporter for a decade and a half, I'd never heard of a woman who had connections with powerful politicians and the mafiosi. A woman who was like a sister to Mastan, someone with the surname Gandhi, who tied a rakhi to a former Prime minister and who had hobnobbed with a powerful Maratha chief minister.

Senile or not, here was Shakoor bhai, the man in the lungi, leading me to this woman's grave. We walk past labyrinthine rows of graves, traversing one end of the graveyard to the other, on the way passing an enclosure—tiflane jannat (the children of heaven)—where young children are buried.

After walking for several minutes, he leads me to the southernmost corner of the graveyard and, stopping near the wall, points towards one particular L-shaped grave, unkempt, decrepit and hidden by thick overgrown bushes.

'Yehi hain unki qabar.' (This is her grave.)

I look at it, but can discern no details. The headstone comprises a plain stone with an inscription which reads: Form No. 2544, Otta No. 601. But it gives no name. I hand Shakoor bhai another fifty-rupee note and am about to tell him he can go, when he resumes talking.

'She was also a freedom fighter—she participated in the freedom struggle against the angrez with Mahatma Gandhi.'

My jaw drops. 'What are you saying? Then how did she become the queen of the underworld?'

'Because Dawood Ibrahim thought of her as his surrogate mother. Also, she was held in high esteem both by the police and the mafia. She had massive clout with all the gangs.'

I slip another bill into his hand and ask, 'Where did she live and operate from?'

'Dongri.'

Dongri is to Mumbai what Palermo is to the Sicilian mafia—at least it was during the Dawood Ibrahim days. And that's when the last piece of the jigsaw puzzle falls into place for me.

'Why, is this Jenabai's grave?'

The old man nods vigorously. 'Haan haan, this is Jenabai's grave.'

I'm puzzled: I've heard about Jenabai, but only that she was a bootlegger and a police informer. The grave-digger had given me a new perspective on this woman.

I'm intrigued; I have to get her story.

Chapter 2

NIGHTCAP AT BAITUL SUROOR

A black Mercedes pulled out of the shed and drove quickly past the small wrought-iron gate of the two- storey villa and onto the winding road. It was June 1980 and the rains had just begun to beat down on the sun-baked city.

Watching the car disappear into the night, he stood there alone, on his balcony. Tense lines creased his forehead. To calm his nerves, he took out a cigarette from the pack of 555 in the pocket of his white kurta. Lighting it, he began to pace the length of the veranda. His villa, the Baitul Suroor, Arabic for 'house of happiness', was situated in one of Mumbai's most expensive areas—Peddar Road.

Finally, over two hours later, seven cigarettes down, he was relieved to see his black Mercedes return and grind to a halt in front of the villa. His driver walked out of the car and opened the back door and an old woman, well in her seventies, stepped out, fidgeting unsteadily with her black umbrella, trying hard to open it, before she got too wet.

Jenabai walked towards the entrance of the villa. The doors had already been left open for her. He hastily stubbed the burning end of his eighth cigarette inside a glass ashtray and rushed downstairs towards the entrance.

He had called her a few hours ago, requesting her to join him for dinner. Hearing the urgency in his voice, she had readily accepted the invitation. His Mercedes had been sent to pick her up from her small home in Dongri at 7 p.m. Passers-by saw her walk out of the building and slip into the car. When she sat in the backseat, the driver exchanged a warm, familiar 'salaam' and then proceeded to drive past the rickety old buildings towards Peddar Road. It had been raining heavily in Dongri, too; however, unlike Peddar Road, Dongri continued to bustle with activity despite the downpour. Protected by blue and black plastic sheets, stalls continued their business as salesmen engaged in their daily routine of drawing customers and selling goods.

The Mercedes stood out in this environment, but Dongri locals knew who was in the car and where she was going. The reason behind the meeting, however, was still a well- kept secret, meant to stay inside the closed walls of Baitul Suroor and revealed only to the one woman who was feared and respected by all in Dongri.

Having reached the villa after around an hour, Jenabai felt surprisingly rejuvenated. The off-white villa was sombre in appearance. Intricately-designed white window grills, stone walls and the humble entrance, with clusters of potted plants, gave outsiders no hint of who lived there, or what he did for a living.

When she entered the house, she saw him standing in anticipation. He was dressed in a white kurta and pyjama. She shut her wet umbrella and placed it inside the bucket at the entrance.

'Salaam Aapa,' he said, referring to her as his elder sister, as he normally did.

'Salaam.'

Then, from the narrow entrance, he directed her towards the spacious drawing room.

'Aapa, it is kind of you to have come here at such short notice,' he said as he led her to one of the sofas.

She gave him a broad smile, although she could sense the discomfort in his voice. She asked for a glass of water and sat back comfortably on the couch, lifting her feet onto the table. He called for someone, who appeared with water in no time. When he had left the room, she said, 'Bhai, you seem to be very disturbed.'

'Aapa ...' he said, and after a long pause continued, 'I have a massive problem. And, whenever I am in some kind of trouble the only person I can think of is you.'

Jenabai was embarrassed, overwhelmed by the influence she possessed over this one man, one of Mumbai's most dangerous personalities, Mastan Haider Mirza. A man whose rags-to-riches story had inspired and been depicted on celluloid time and again.

Legend had it that Mastan was originally from Chennai

and had come to Mumbai in 1934, along with his father. He had started off as a mechanic, repairing cycles before moving to the Mumbai docks as a coolie in 1944. There his job was to unload huge boxes and containers from ships coming from Aden, Dubai, Hong Kong. In the years to come, he made millions of rupees from smuggling gold, silver ingots and electronic goods and, along with Karim Lala and Vardharajan Mudaliar, went on to form one of the most formidable gangs in Mumbai. His villa, his Mercedes and his tremendous influence, were all off-shoots of the enormous wealth he had hoarded illegally over the years.

Now, here *she* was, Jenabai, in Mastan's house, discussing his problems, counselling him ... Jenabai could not have felt more pride in being called his sister.

Chapter 3

THE BEGINNINGS OF THE SCHEMER

Born in the early 1920s to a Muslim Memon Halai family, Zainab, alias Jenabai, was one among six siblings. Her father made ends meet ferrying passengers on Victoria carriages across the city, and the family lived in a one-room tenement on Mohammad Ali Road, Dongri, in Mumbai.

Dongri, a stone's throw away from the cloth market in Kalbadevi, was initially part of the original island of Mumbai, which stretched from Malabar Hill to the Dongri hills. Mumbai, at the time, was divided into seven islands, which included Colaba, Old Woman Island, Mahim, Parel, Worli and Mazgaon. In the mid-1700s, the Dongri hills were levelled as part of the plan to merge the different islands of Mumbai. After the hills were levelled, the low-lying patch of uneven land between Crawford Market in the north and the reclaimed lands of Kamathipura in the south came to be called Dongri.

Today, Dongri—choc-a-block with rickety, old

Mumbai was Daana Bazaar at Masjid Bunder, close to Dongri. In need of quick money to sustain her family, Jenabai started working as a broker for smuggled grain, playing intermediary to wholesalers and dealers of lentils, pulses, sugar and basmati rice. Jenabai would procure foodgrain in bulk from the wholesalers at Daana Bazaar on a commission, and then sell this grain to dealers who would sell it for a higher price and give her a margin of the profits. She also sold grain to people who lived with her in the tenement. Hoarding and trading in grain without a licence was illegal and punishable by law. The police raided Jenabai's room at Chunawala building several times but never managed to get enough evidence to book her.

Since she was a Memon, she was also fluent in Gujarati, making it easier for her to interact with the wholesalers and traders, most of whom belonged to the Gujarati community. These Gujarati traders soon began to refer to her as 'sister' or Jenaben. Since her dealings were mostly in rice (chaaval), the title 'Chaavalwaali' (one who deals in rice) became suffixed to her name, and locals in Dongri and Daana Bazaar began calling her Jenabai Chaavalwaali.

Chapter 4

AT THE DINNER TABLE

Mastan hadn't said a word for several minutes. Jenabai didn't push him. Quietly, she sipped the last of her ginger tea—her third cup—from the saucer.

Suddenly, his face tense, he said, 'I need help Aapa, this is very important for me.'

Bringing her feet down from the glass table, Jenabai lifted herself from the couch. 'Bhai, what is the matter ... I have been sitting here for such a long time,' she said, pushing her feet into her gold-heeled sandals.

'Let's talk about it over food,' he said.

Her white chikan kurta had creased slightly, and the dupatta that covered her reddish-brown mehendi-dyed hair had shifted position. She tidied her kurta, straightened her dupatta and walked towards the mahogany dining table. She had a regal air about her, her ears glinting with diamond-studded earrings and her hands heavy with the weight of gold bangles.

The dining table was laden with food, from mutton korma and pulao, kebabs to murg musalam. Mastan sat across the dining table from Jenabai. The domestic help started serving her, looking at her intermittently to check if she wanted more. She nodded.

The help obliged her and then went towards Mastan with a bowl of pulao. Mastan shook his head. 'Not now,' he said.

'You won't eat?' she asked.

'I prefer cigarettes for now,' he replied.

As she began to eat, he started to speak slowly, forming each of his sentences in his head before he voiced them aloud.

'Aapa, I want to leave this illegal business.'

'Why?' she asked, surprised.

'I have spent most of the last few years either behind bars or making endless rounds of the court. Narayan bhai (Janata Party leader Jaiprakash Narayan) helped in my release only after I promised him that I would become clean,' he said. 'I have been contemplating doing something else for a long time but nothing has worked in my favour.'

Jenabai heard him out patiently.

The last six to seven years had been very difficult for Mastan. First, in 1974, he had been detained under the Maintenance of Internal Security Act (MISA) for ninety days. Following this, the government arrested Mastan under the Conservation of Foreign Exchange and Prevention of Smuggling Act. Then, during the Emergency in 1977, he, along with other gangsters like Karim Lala, was once again tried under MISA. In fact, Jenabai had also been jailed under MISA; however, the charges against her could not be proved.

MISA was a controversial law that was originally passed by the Indian Parliament in 1971, during the administration of Prime Minister Indira Gandhi. Indira Gandhi had introduced the Act with the main objective of providing law enforcement agencies with powers of indefinite 'preventive' detention of individuals, search and seizure of property without warrants. Despite hiring the best criminal lawyers like Ram Jethmalani, Mastan languished behind bars during the entire Emergency. He realised that he no longer wielded the influence that he had enjoyed in Mumbai as a smuggler. Also, the endless legal battles had pushed him into debt.

When the Emergency was lifted and the Janata Party came to power in 1979, Mastan pleaded with Jaiprakash Narayan to intervene with the then prime minister, Morarji Desai, to show compassion towards him. Mastan had filed affidavits and under oath, sworn to the government that he would try to turn over a new leaf. His plea was accepted and he was finally released from detention.

'I am sinking in a sea of debt, Aapa ... I have to repay loans, my house has been mortgaged. The only possible business ventures where I can now invest money are real estate or the movies,' Mastan said.

'There are a lot of risks in investing money in movies,'

Jenabai said, but her thoughts lingered on the memory of this man that had been embedded in her mind several years ago. She remembered how much in awe of him she had been when she was first introduced to him by the Mumbai-based Tamilian don Vardharajan Mudaliar. He had been so much braver then, so much larger than life ...

Chapter 5

FROM CHAAVALWALI TO DAARUWALI

Prohibition had always been central to Mahatma Gandhi's and the Congress' agenda. Hence, on 1 August 1939, two years after the first Congress ministry was created in the Bombay province, prohibition was introduced in the city. However, law-enforcers faced problems in the very first week of implementing it. For one whole week, there were clashes between groups for and against prohibition.

The home minister at the time, Barrister K.M. Munshi, carried out an intensive recruitment programme in the police force to implement the Prohibition Act effectively. An exclusive cadre called the X Division was created and was headed by a DCP, Prohibition. New sub-inspectors were also trained for special prohibition duty, and men from the Excise Department were brought into the city police department.

However, when the Second World War broke out in 1939, the mammoth prohibition force was diverted for security measures to the docks and the implementation of prohibition suffered.

In 1946, after the Nazis were defeated, the Congress government came back to power and prohibition was imposed on Mumbai again. Veteran politician and then chief minister of the Bombay province Morarji Desai, who was staunchly against the selling and consumption of alcohol, declared complete prohibition in liquor sales in Bombay from 6 April 1950, by passing the Bombay Prohibition Act of 1949. Before this order fell into place, the Christian and Koli communities distilled their own liquor, like jambul, jira, moha etc., while most of the other alcohol available was imported from the West, particularly England.

Unfortunately, prohibition did nothing but sow the seeds for bigger crimes in Mumbai, opening the gateway for bootleggers and smugglers. Apart from these, a number of 'aunty joints' also sprung up to quench the thirst of the alcohol-deprived population. Poor Goan Christian women brewed liquor in their backyards and kitchen, and sold it discreetly for a good price. Since their patrons found it difficult to pronounce their names, they were nicknamed according to their physical attributes like Gori Aunty, Chikni Aunty and Baidewali Aunty. Bootlegging was seen as a most lucrative businesses with profits running into thousands of rupees, and these aunty joints soon went on to become part of the Mumbai culture.

It was during this time that Jenabai Chaavalwali remarried an already married Iqbal Gandhi. She was still illegally dealing in grain but the profits were marginal and she was tired of making minuscule amounts. That was when she met Tamilian don Vardharajan Muniswami Mudaliar.

One evening, Jenabai—like several other ardent devotees—had gone to visit the 260-year-old shrine of Bismillah Shah Baba at the Chhatrapati Shivaji Terminus. When she was about to leave, she saw a burly, dark man, in his mid-thirties distributing niyaz, sacred food, to devotees in the dargah. Jenabai had heard a lot about the benevolence of this man from her neighbours in Dongri. Though he was a Hindu, his generosity at the dargah had been spoken of. She decided to stay back and meet this man, on the pretext of taking her share of niyaz before leaving.

After the man completed his rounds, he sat for some time outside the shrine, chatting with the regulars and acquaintances. Jenabai approached him and began crying about her financial situation, and how she was struggling to make ends meet. 'I want you to help me, Bhai,' she pleaded. 'My husband does not work. Feeding my children and looking after the household is solely my responsibility ... I tried my hands in the grain business for a few years but I could not earn enough. I really don't know what to do. You are a big man, everyone respects you ... if you could give me a small job, God will bless you.'

The man, affectionately called Vardha, sat silently

listening to her. Her wily tone made him foresee a bankable option for his bootlegging and liquor business. After prohibition, Vardharajan—like many others—had decided to start his own local, illicit liquor trade. For this, he had also set up base in the marshy lands of central Mumbai and got his men to start brewing their own liquor.

After a long pause, Vardha took a deep breath and asked, 'Will you get into the liquor business?'

'Bhai, what are you saying? It would be against my qaum. I cannot do it.'

'Listen, who is asking you to drink the daaru? I know so many Muslims in this line of work. Your religion doesn't stop you from getting into the business. Does it?' he asked. 'Daaru ke dhande mein bahut paisa hain (the liquor business is very lucrative). Everyone, right from housewives to big businessmen, is into it and all of them are trying to make a quick buck from the government's foolish policy.'

Jenabai did not say a word.

He continued, 'Trust me, even I felt the same initially but today I am minting crores. God has been kind to me, which is why I am showing my gratitude by coming here every week. You can work in this business line and still be a good Muslim.'

'What will I have to do?' she asked.

'See, I have this piece of land at Antop Hill. My men brew liquor there. Your job will be to sell this concentrated liquor. The profits will be divided equally between you and me.' Jenabai was still unconvinced. 'How much will I make … if …?'

'That depends on how much you sell. Maybe thousands, sometimes even lakhs.' Jenabai thought about it for some time, balancing the pros and cons in her head. 'And the risks involved?' she asked.

Vardha smirked, 'Don't worry about that. You just need to know how to deal with the police.'

Finally, Jenabai's face lit up and her jawline stretched as she broke into a cunning smile.

With Vardha's help, Jenabai got into the bootlegging business in the early 1960s. Her Maharashtrian neighbour, Vicky bhai, soon went on to become her sidekick and financial manager in the trade. Jenabai's age, experience and, most importantly, her ability to handle and manipulate the police, helped her grow swiftly in the business. Before long, Jenabai—now known as Jenabai Daaruwali—became one of Vardha's closest aides.

Meanwhile, Vardha's clout continued to increase. Press reports during the 1960s pegged his trade in illicit liquor to around Rs 12 crore a year. But Vardha wanted more—and the most lucrative business was considered to be the smuggling of gold. He could not break into the business alone, however: the Muslim dons—who had the right contacts in the Gulf—had the monopoly on it. So Vardha befriended dons like Mastan and Karim Lala, and they bonded to form a strong force. This was when Vardha first introduced Jenabai Daaruwali to Mastan.

Chapter 6

THE PROBLEM

It was 10 p.m., and the rains had become fiercer than before, covering the sky with a cloud of gloom.

Jenabai had finished eating the sumptuous dinner and was resting on the three-seater. Mastan had started pacing the floor in the drawing room.

'Sit down,' she told him, moving from her reclining position to give him some space. 'Let us get to discussing the real problem.'

'I have been thinking about getting into the real estate business for a very long time and have been eyeing a huge property on Belassis Road in Bombay Central,' he said, as he dug inside the pocket of his kurta for a lighter.

'So ...'

'The land is owned by the Chiliyas and they are refusing to budge,' he said, lighting another cigarette. 'That plot is a gold mine, Aapa. If I get my hands on it, I will not only be able to repay all my debts, zindagi bhi set ho jaayegi (I'll also be set for life).'

Jenabai knew how much it must have cost Mastan to admit his helplessness in resolving the issue. He was always conscious of his public image—perhaps because he was defensive about his lack of education—and hated to appear anything but wise.

'What does Karim bhai have to say about this?' she asked. 'I spoke to him some time ago. But he told me that he may not be able to help this time around because it is beyond his capacity.'

'Why?' Jenabai asked.

'At my behest, Karim bhai had sent some of his men to settle the matter. All the men came back with broken arms and legs. Aapa, these Chiliyas are way too powerful. We are just too small for them.'

The Chiliyas—Gujarati Muslims from Banaskantha district—were a very strong force. Usually in the hotel or real estate business, they were fiercely committed to protecting themselves and what they perceived as theirs.

Jenabai smiled. She looked around the drawing room and then lifted her fragile body from the sofa and walked towards the side table where pens and paper lay. Picking up a red ball pen and a sheet of paper, she came back, sat beside him and asked him if he would help her solve a riddle. Mastan was annoyed; he felt like he was being mocked. He did not reply but she continued, unperturbed.

Being illiterate, Jenabai had rarely used a pen. Today,

she placed the piece of paper on the table, hesitantly held the red pen tightly in her right fist and drew a long vertical line in the centre of the blank page.

Then, lifting her head, she said, 'Can you make this line smaller without touching it?'

Mastan was flummoxed. In a fit of rage, he punched the cushion of his sofa, and said, 'Aapa, I have been mentally disturbed for weeks and instead of helping me out, you are asking me to solve this stupid riddle of yours.'

Jenabai smirked and then, pointing one of her gold-ringed fingers towards her head, she said, 'Think Mastan bhai, think. The solution to all your problems lies in this riddle.'

Mastan's anger slowly began to subside. His eyes shifted to the paper on the table. He looked at it blankly for some time and then, in a perplexed tone asked, 'How?'

She broke into laughter, again held the pen in her fist and began to draw a bigger line beside the existing one. Then, lifting her head, she said, 'See, it is so simple. If this line is big and you cannot erase it, just draw a bigger line next to it.'

Mastan wasn't sure what was on Jenabai's mind. But he knew that his faith in her had never been misplaced. She was shrewd enough to let go without giving him a solution. She had drawn the path. He had only to walk on it ...

Chapter 7

BOOTLEGGER TURNS INFORMER

Jenabai thrived during the prohibition. She amassed enormous wealth as a bootlegger and was quick to learn the tricks of the trade under Vardharajan, Mastan and Karim Lala.

Her closeness to some of the city's most hardcore smugglers enhanced Jenabai's importance by leaps and bounds. People would often approach her for advice and help in settling disputes. This, and the increase in her wealth, gave her confidence, and she became abusive and overbearing.

During this time, Jenabai also developed friendly relations with the police. Police constable Ibrahim Kaskar and his wife Aamina, Dawood Ibrahim's parents, were like family to her. Their children treated her like a second mother.

This was the same time when the government and the police were again trying to implement prohibition effectively across the city. Besides the X Division, which had been introduced by former home minister Barrister K.M. Munshi way back in 1939, a special Prohibition Intelligence Section was created. The Prohibition Intelligence Section was headquartered at Palton Road (where Haj House stands today) and was responsible for effectively implementing 'daaru-bandi' in the city.

The police learned about Jenabai's bootlegging business and raided her room several times but did not manage to gather anything from such raids, simply because she knew how to manipulate people. She would often place photographs of gods and goddesses in the corner of her room. All her liquor stock would be hidden in a chest or box below those photos and the police, during their raids, would assume that the space was sacred and refrain from searching that area properly.

However, after facing severe criticism for being lackadaisical about Jenabai's illegal business, the special Prohibition Intelligence Section finally arrested her and she served a few weeks in jail.

In 1962, based on a tip-off, two determined police officers, sub-inspectors in the X Division, Coovershaw Dinshaw Bhesadia and Ramakant Temkar, managed to break into her house and catch her red-handed—finally busting one of the biggest liquor mafia scams of the time. After scanning all the rooms in the building, the officers finally found illicit liquor hidden in the water tank of Jenabai's aide, Vicky's room.

In 1964, sub-inspector C.D. Bhesadia was rewarded by the then Mumbai Police Commissioner S. Majeedullah for his services and later, became one of the most talented detectives in the Anti-Corruption Bureau, retiring as assistant commissioner of police, Crime Branch. Ironically, Jenabai later went on to become a key khabri, or informer, for Bhesadia.

Unconfirmed accounts state that after her arrest, Jenabai approached the then chief minister Yashwantrao Chavan with grievances of harassment by the Pydhonie and V.P. Road police. She is said to have played on her poverty, her children and how she was trying to make ends meet. What transpired at the meeting between the two is still unclear; however, after the meeting, Dongri's most fearless woman apparently moved on to become a police informant.

After her stint in jail, Jenabai realised that if she had to be a real player in the market, she would have to keep both the law enforcers and the ganglords happy. Jenabai's smuggling know-how made her a valuable informant, and, at the time, informants were offered ten per cent of the total worth of the goods seized. However, cunning as always, Jenabai did not stop her bootlegging and grain business.

As an informant, she daringly visited the houses of police officers after midnight in a burqa. Families of police officers, for whom she was a key informant, would address her as Hirabai, because they saw her visit their homes wearing diamond-studded nose rings and earrings.

Another police informant, who still lives in Dongri and runs a shop of his own, explained how Jenabai would juggle the interests of the police and the mafia. 'If illegal items were being smuggled from seven different ports in the city, Jenabai, who knew about all seven, would drop the names of only one or two. The police would seize the goods and then give her part of the valued amount without realising that she was aware of the others, as well,' he said. And since it was only a couple from the seven that they knew Jenabai was aware of, the dons believed she had nothing to do with the raids. Thus, she remained a favourite of Mastan and Lala.

Ironically, Jenabai—who had accumulated immense wealth through tip-offs—lost her most prized treasure because she didn't learn in time about the plot to murder her youngest son, Kamaal Darwesh.

Kamaal, at twenty-four, was not only an aggressive youth, but an extremely arrogant one too. Like his mother, he was also heavily involved in illegal businesses, but his attitude paved the way for his downfall, since the Mumbai mafia began to feel that Kamaal had become too big-headed. One morning, four men stabbed Kamaal to death a few metres from Jenabai's house near Minara Masjid in Dongri. Jenabai was not in town at the time. The news of the death of her youngest son came as a big shock, mentally crippling her.

She took to her bed, crying profusely day and night, cursing and blaming her clout for his death. For the next six months, she visited his grave every day, sitting beside his tomb and praying for his soul. Then her attention turned to the men responsible for her son's death. She left no stone unturned to track down the four men. Sorrow had taken over her life, and so had this obsession. Finally, Mastan and Lala, concerned about Jenabai, decided to take four men to her and tell her that these were her son's murderers. The men were made to sit in front of her and then Mastan and Lala proceeded to dissuade her from taking any action against them or going to the police. After much coaxing and religious arguments, Jenabai decided to forgive the men who had allegedly killed her son.

Chapter 8

THE SIMPLE SUBTERFUGE

Mastan had deliberately left the windows ajar so that the cold, wet breeze could enter the drawing room. He was still smoking his cigarette, glancing now and then at the two lines Jenabai had drawn on the paper that lay on the centre table. By now Jenabai was sitting on the floor, where she felt most comfortable.

Pointing to the bigger line, Jenabai said, 'This line represents a bigger force. A force that you will create.'

'A bigger force?' he asked.

Jenabai made herself a paan and said, 'Yes, you will prepare a bigger force against the Chiliyas.'

'Where the hell can I create such a force from?'

'What are the Ibrahim brothers and the Pathan gang for?' she asked, chewing the paan. 'Get them together.'

At the time, the Pathan gangsters—Amirzada, Alamzeb, Shehzada, Samad Khan—and the then underdogs, the Ibrahim brothers Dawood and Sabir, were the two major warring factions, constantly involved in gun battles. The incessant bloodshed caused by the gang war had, in fact, become a great cause of concern for Mastan and his friend Karim Lala, the stalwarts of Mumbai's underworld.

And from what Mastan could understand, Jenabai wanted him to bring these two gangs together as one force against the Chiliyas.

'This is no solution, Aapa!' Mastan said, astonished. An alliance comprising the Ibrahim brothers and the Pathans meant calling a truce, which in the present scenario was impossible. For Mastan, even bringing them together into one room seemed an unlikely scenario.

'Bhai, if you get them together, it will only help you,' she said. 'The Pathans are a strong force to reckon with in VP and Grant Road, while Ibrahim's sons have a stronghold in Nagpada. And the Belassis Road property that you have your eyes on lies exactly in the centre of Grant Road, VP Road and Nagpada.'

Mastan was surprised at Jenabai's observation. 'Hmm ... that is true.'

'Imagine, if you all unite to become one force, even the government will stand no chance against you. The force will not only help you get the property but also ensure that it is well protected.'

The odds of calling a truce were still close to zero but Mastan realised that this was probably his only option.

'I can request Karim bhai to convince the Pathans. But what about Ibrahim bhai's sons? They will never agree to this. Even Ibrahim bhai is fed up; he has no control over them.'

Dawood Ibrahim, a young man in his twenties at this time, was just another wannabe gangster, trying to make it big in the underworld. A resident of Mussafir Khana near Dongri junction, Dawood indulged in petty extortion, along with his brother Sabir. He was trying hard to get the attention of the mafia bigwigs; often, in order to evade the police, he was forced to go into hiding.

'I will handle the Ibrahim brothers. Dawood and Sabir are like my sons. They won't refuse if I speak to them,' she said.

'Aapa, it is not as easy as you are making it sound. At the end of the day, how will you convince them to become a united group?' Mastan asked.

Jenabai smiled. She knew the one thing that bound them all. 'Bhai, think carefully,' she said. 'These people are morons. They have been fighting without any real motive, like goons, allowing others to take advantage of them. But, even though their egos are bloated like air balloons, their weaknesses can bring them down. And to our good fortune, there is this one weakness which is common to us all. Their ambitions and powers can divide them, but in the end, they belong to that one same world.'

'It would save so much of time if you put all this in plain words for me,' Mastan said, agitated.

'Hmm ... it is simple. See, we all believe in one God, we know the teachings of one Prophet,' she said.

'That is all rubbish. None of them actually follow the teachings of Islam,' Mastan said.

'You hit the nail on the head. Ultimately, these men are all hypocrites. They won't follow the right path that our religion has laid down for us, but are ever willing to don the garb of protectors of Islam and shed blood in the name of God. Invoke the name of religion—a truce will follow,' Jenabai said.

For the first time, Mastan felt small in front of Jenabai. She not only made things seem possible, what she had said was something that had never struck him before.

He was still doubtful though. 'We have to figure out a way to bring all of them under one roof ...' he said.

'Don't worry. Everything will be fine; I will ensure that it is made possible.'

'Can I trust you with this?' he asked.

'Do you still have doubts, Bhai?' she asked, shaking her head as she rose from the floor. 'I need to go now. It is quite late.'

Mastan called for his black Mercedes and walked Jenabai to the car. As the car left Baitul Suroor, the lights in the villa gradually dimmed and faded to black.

Chapter 9

THE VERSATILE PLOTTER

The sun on her face woke Jenabai. She made an attempt to turn away from it but the brightness in the room killed her desire to sleep any further. She finally got up at 9.30 in the morning. None of her children or grandchildren were at home, she knew. She peeped outside through the large square window of her Dongri room. Jenabai still hung on to her tiny house despite having so much money, because she was attached to it.

Cars, buses and two-wheelers moved at a fair pace and it was routine business at the shopping stalls below. The roads were dry and there wasn't the slightest indication of the previous evening's downpour. Someone from below called out to her, 'Jenamaasi, salaam!' She returned the greeting and returned inside; she was in no mood to engage in small talk. She had suffered a sleepless night and the restlessness was making her head spin.

She realised that she had made a heavy promise

to Mastan, and she was already feeling its burden on her shoulders. Jenabai was not used to making empty assurances to the people she cared for. And though she might have convinced Mastan that she was able to handle the situation at hand, she knew that convincing Dawood and Sabir would be difficult.

She decided to make herself some tea. She took a small vessel, filled it with water and placed it on the stove to boil.

Jenabai looked at the framed inscription of a saying from the Koran that hung on the wall opposite her kitchen and closed her eyes for a fraction of a second. She had already decided to try her best, but left it to God to show her a way out.

When the water was boiling, Jenabai spooned tea and sugar into the vessel. She turned the gas stove off and was about to pour out the tea when she heard a loud knock on the door of her room.

'Maasi, open the door,' a young voice said.

Recognising the voice, she placed the vessel back on the stove, got hold of her dupatta and moved towards the door, opening it slowly. Dawood stood there; he was sweating profusely.

Without saying a word, he entered the room with a familiarity that revealed how often he visited her home. He went towards the sink and rinsed his face. Jenabai, meanwhile, made a conscious attempt to compose herself.

'Oy, chhokra, what's happened now?' she asked, referring to the sullen look on Dawood's face.

'Don't ask. Just one of those usual fights but the man is badly hurt,' he said.

'Whom did you beat up?' she asked.

'Maasi, it was that notorious Hamid Chuha from Manish Market. The man had become a big menace. You know we've been fighting for control over some of those shops. I went to sort things out with him today, but this time he really got out of hand and I beat him up.'

'Hmm ... good. So you evened things out finally.'

'But now I am in trouble, Maasi ... Chuha is in the ICU and the dress-wallahs (the police) are after me ... my father also knows about it and he won't spare me either. I don't want to be beaten up by him. Please help me Maasi, get me out of this situation.'

Jenabai sat silently for some time, trying to sort out the whole issue in her head. Suddenly, the wheels in her mind started turning and she said, 'No one will dare to harm you in my presence. But I hope you realise that it won't be easy for me to convince both the police and your father at the same time.'

'I know only one thing—however difficult things are, nothing is impossible for you.'

Jenabai gave him a small smile. 'I may need a favour from you sometime soon. Will you agree to do it for me?'

Without the slightest hesitation Dawood agreed. 'Maasi, I am ready to lay down my life for you. You are like my mother.'

'So leave it on me then. But for now, just stay put at my place,' she said.

'No, Maasi, it is not safe. I will come and meet you tomorrow. Would you be able to sort things out for me by then?'

'Come tomorrow, we will see ...' she replied, handing him a towel to wipe his face.

Later in the evening, Jenabai made an unexpected visit to Mussafir Khana. Dawood's father, Ibrahim Kaskar, was sitting on the single bed at the end of the room with his hand on his head; tense, angry—and yet an air of fragility hung about him because of his age. The atmosphere in the room was solemn when Jenabai entered the room.

'Salaam Jenabai, come in. How come you are here?' he asked. She entered and sat on the small stool in the room.

'Salaam. Ibrahim bhai, I heard about Dawood, so I thought I'd come and meet you. Has he come home?'

Ibrahim turned red. 'He won't dare to come home. Dawood has left me ashamed. I had so much respect among the police fraternity and he has stripped me of it.'

She heard him out patiently, allowing him to vent his frustration. Aamina came in with some tea for Jenabai. Both the women hugged. 'Our bad days are here, Aapa. Dawood has done it again,' Aamina said, crying as she released herself from Jenabai's embrace.

'Don't cry, your son is not at fault, he is a nice boy,' Jenabai said.

'What are you saying? At least don't support him. That Hamid Chuha is suffering in the ICU; he is caught between life and death. The police has already come here twice. It is such shame, everyone is talking about it,' Ibrahim said angrily.

'Arrey Ibrahim bhai, don't talk about that Hamid Chuha—he is a very bad man. It is actually good if he dies. He has troubled so many people. Our Dawood had just gone to sort out matters with him. But it was he who started beating him up. Whatever Dawood did was in self- defence.'

'How do you know so much, Jenabai?' Ibrahim asked suspiciously.

'Dawood is like my son. The moment I heard about the incident, I first thought about you and Aamina bi. I enquired with some boys who were present at the shop when the fight took place between them. They told me that it was not Dawood's fault.'

'By the grace of God, my son is innocent,' Aamina said when she heard this.

Ibrahim was not as easily convinced. 'Jenabai, we need two hands to clap. I have seen so many such fights during my service and I know that my son is not innocent.'

'Bhai, Dawood was beaten really badly. If he did not defend himself, we would have been attending his funeral today. Would you choose Hamid Chuha over Dawood?'

Ibrahim did not say anything for a long time. Then: 'If this is the case, I would like to speak with Dawood. He can't afford to repeat such a thing again.'

'I will try and track him down and tell him to meet you. Just don't be harsh with him. He is a nice boy and you can trust me. I would have killed to have such a son.' Saying this, Jenabai walked out of the room.

Feeling confident that she had sorted out half of Dawood's problem—his fear of what his father would do to him—Jenabai turned her mind to the other half. The men who could put Dawood behind bars. His track record and unpopularity with the police department was a known fact and Jenabai knew that if she had to turn things in her favour, she would have to go directly to someone with power.

The next day Jenabai made a trip to the Crime Branch office at the Mumbai Police Headquarters in Crawford Market. She had decided to meet one of the most reputed and distinguished senior Crime Branch officers.

Tall, burly and well-built, the officer was considered a taskmaster in his time. Having served in the Crime Branch for years, he knew its ways well. As an informant, Jenabai had always maintained cordial relations with the officer.

The officer was at his desk when one of his constables rang him about Jenabai. Surprised, he asked the constable to call her in.

'Come in Jenabai. Salaam. What brings you here today?' the officer asked.

'I was going to buy some vegetables from the market so I thought I'd just drop by to meet you.'

'Well, that's good. It means I get to finally meet you after months because of your vegetables,' he joked.

'Sahib, I sing your praises to people almost everyday.

I even tell my people that the police force hasn't seen a better officer,' she said.

After a few more minutes of small talk, Jenabai decided to get to the point. 'Sahib, I feel bad for you. These gang wars in the city are keeping all you dress-wallahs busy.'

'Yes, we have a big task at hand. In fact, it was only yesterday that Dawood and his goons beat up a shop owner from Manish Market. That man's condition is very serious and that haraami Dawood is absconding.'

'Did you go to his home? He must be hiding there,' she said.

'Usko paagal kutte ne kaata hai kya? (Has he gone mad?) He won't dare to sit at home. Our officers are watching his house anyway, but that boy is too clever, he won't go there. I feel bad for his father sometimes. Look at him and look at his son.'

Jenabai did not say anything. She knew what was coming.

'By the way, if I am not mistaken, you know their family well, right?' the officer enquired.

Jenabai suppressed a smile. This was going to be much simpler than she had thought it would be.

'Well ... our families are very close ... all of us, including Dawood.'

'Hmm ... yes, I was wondering if you could help us out.'

Jenabai stiffened and said, 'Sahib, what are you saying! This will be next to impossible for me. I can part with any amount of information, but how can I tell you the whereabouts of someone whose family is close to me.'

The officer was all attention immediately. 'Does that mean you know where Dawood is?

'No ... I don't.'

'But you just said—'

'I don't know where he is at the moment but Dawood does listen to me. He treats me like his mother. I may also be able track him down ... but ... but, this will come at a price.'

The officer was taken aback. This woman had the nerve to lay down conditions in front of a senior Crime Branch officer! Calming down, he asked, 'And what will you do for me?'

'What if I make Dawood your informant?'

'Informant?' the officer asked, shocked.

'Well, I am sure you know what it would be, to make Dawood an informant. He is an upcoming gangster, and his knowledge of the underworld is indisputable. Also, he has the reputation of being sincere to the cause of the underworld. No one will doubt him.' She paused to let that sink in, and then continued, 'If you make him an informant, you can also keep a check on his own activities and in the process clip his wings before he learns to fly.'

The officer didn't say anything for a few minutes. Then he asked, 'And what would the price be for this?'

'Nothing ... Just drop all charges against him,' she said.

'Are you out of your mind, Jenabai?' he shouted,

adding, 'I respect you but that does not mean you can take advantage of my goodness. I won't drop any charges against him … never.'

'Is that your final word, Sahib?'

The officer did not reply. Picking up a file, he pretended to be engrossed in what he was reading. Watching him behave this way, Jenabai decided to walk out, half-dejected and hopeful at the same time. When she opened the door to leave his room, the officer, without looking up from his file, said softly, 'I will need time.'

'How much time?' she asked.

'This is no joke … I will take my time.'

'So should I presume you won't harm him till then?' she asked.

The officer did not speak.

'I will fulfil my promise, I hope you will too,' she said and walked out, pleased with herself.

Unexpectedly, Dawood did not turn up at her place that day. Jenabai was eager to break the news about his father and the police to him. She also felt it was a good time to talk to him about the meeting she and Mastan had planned. When there was no sign of Dawood, she decided to have dinner and go to sleep.

At around 3.40 a.m., she heard a faint knock on her door. Assuming she was imagining things, she ignored it. Half-a-minute later, she heard another knock on the door. A soft voice said, 'Jenamaasi, Dawood here.'

Jenabai moved to the door, opening it quietly, careful not to wake her son who was also sleeping in the room.

'Maasi, any luck?' Dawood asked.

'What do you think?' Jenabai smiled. 'Your maasi has managed everything, now you are a free bird and I've spoken with your father as well. Just be careful for some time though, the dress-wallahs as usual have not given me a full assurance,' she said.

'I will handle that,' he said.

A very relieved Dawood drank the glass of water offered and was ready to leave when Jenabai stopped him.

'Now it is your turn,' she said.

'Oh! Yes, of course. What do you want me to do, Maasi?'

'Mastan bhai is tired of your gang war. You boys have caused a lot of commotion in Dongri. Do you realise that you all are fighting against your own brothers?'

Dawood remained silent, so Jenabai continued, 'Mastan wants the Pathans and you all to unite and become one strong force, so that nobody takes us lightly. For this, he wants to have a joint meeting with you all.'

'Maasi, I won't come. I do not want bloodshed in Mastan bhai's house.'

'Nothing of that sort will ever happen in my presence. You promised me, now you can't back out. Just get Sabir and come. I will let you know when ...'

Dawood was in a tight spot. He did not want to be part of the meeting—but he had given her his word.

And so Jenabai had her way.

Chapter 10

MASTAN'S MASTERSTROKE

Mumbai's warring gangsters finally met at Mastan's bungalow in the wet month of July.

On that particular day, Jenabai had been at Mastan's home since dawn. Apart from Mastan, the domestic help and her, no one else was present in the house.

After a series of intense discussions with Karim Lala, the three had drawn the final list of invitees for the meeting that was going to be held that night.

As part of a mutual understanding, everyone was requested not to carry any sort of weapon to prevent the chance bloodshed.

The worry on Mastan's face was apparent as the time for the guests' arrival approached. Though Jenabai tried to assure him of a good outcome, he was unsure about what would actually ensue from the meeting.

The visitors started pouring in by late evening. Jenabai was not as concerned about the others as she was about

Dawood and Sabir. To suppress the duo's volatility, Jenabai had specifically asked Mastan to call her close friend and their father Ibrahim Kaskar, for the meeting. Finally, they were all there: the Pathan chief Karim Lala and his gang, Dawood, Sabir and their father, Majid Kalia, Hussain Somji, Dilip Aziz, Hanif—all sitting in cold silence.

The fact that Jenabai was the only woman there, sitting amongst them and chatting comfortably with the men, said much about her influence and the respect that she was accorded in the underworld at the time.

When the meeting was set to begin, Jenabai went and sat beside Dawood, holding his clenched fist—in some way trying to convey to him the importance of maintaining his cool throughout.

Mastan finally stubbed his cigarette out in the glass ashtray on the dining table and approached his visitors.

'It gives me great pride to see my brothers sit together under one roof today. There has been a lot of bad blood and misunderstanding between us. But I want all of us to be one again and I have chosen my home to be the humble ground for this reunion,' Mastan said. No one in the room spoke. Jenabai, however, threw smiling glances at each and every person in the room.

Mastan looked at the faces of each of his visitors and said, 'We are all Muslims, and though we believe in the same religion, we have failed to identify our common enemy. Instead, we indulge in in-fighting and bloodshed, killing our own brothers. We have made a mockery of our faith and have made fools of ourselves. Everyone is laughing, including the government and the police.'

'Very well said, Mastan bhai. We have become jokers. The government thinks we can harm no one except our own brothers. Yah Allah ... what have we made of ourselves?' Jenabai contributed her bit.

'This is nonsense. We have always cared for other Muslims. In fact, we never initiate attacks. We cannot help it if others consider themselves superior and try to crush every step we take,' Dawood said.

The Pathans immediately stood up. 'You think we consider ourselves superior? Now, you kids will teach us how to do our work? Let's settle this now, once and for all, and you will soon know who is superior,' one of the Pathan's men said, drawing his pistol.

Dawood's brother Sabir rose in a fit of rage and was preparing to attack when Jenabai got up in anger. 'We strictly instructed you not to carry that gun. This is Mastan bhai's home, not a battlefield. You men can do what you want outside his house, not here.' She turned to Dawood and stared expressionlessly at him.

Realising the consequences Sabir's behaviour could have, Dawood caught hold of him and asked him to sit.

Mastan, relieved that Jenabai had managed to control the situation, said, 'For the sake of Allah and Islam, let us resolve our differences. Let us take an oath that we shall refrain from targeting each other in future.'

Jenabai got up almost immediately and covered her

head with her white dupatta as if in prayer and went into the next room. The visitors sat tensely, wondering where she had gone. Moments later, she came out with a Koran which was covered in a dark green cloth. She placed it carefully on the side table and came and sat with the guests. One of the visitors asked his boys to place the Koran on the centre table.

'Let us take an oath on the Koran,' Mastan said.

Jenabai encouraged Dawood and Sabir to place their hands on the holy book; once they did, others slowly followed. Putting their hands out, the men softly muttered that they would abstain from killing their brothers and live peacefully and in total harmony.

Soon after this meeting, Mastan let them in on the problem he was facing on Belassis Road. The Pathans and Dawood's gang met the tenants and ordered them to vacate the land. The Chiliyas fought fearlessly; however, they couldn't stand up to the joint might of the two gangs and they finally lost their land. Mastan then went on to build a tall, multi-storied building on the same plot.

It was a historic peace pact in the history of the Mumbai underworld, engineered by Mastan at his house and whose chief architect, undisputably, was Jenabai.

Chapter 11

TWELVE YEARS LATER–THE GANDHIAN'S MARCH

It was January 1993, just a few years before the island city of Bombay became Mumbai.

Mumbai, the city of dreams, which had always been seen as a smorgasbord of diverse religions, was suddenly shrouded by the communal shadows of the past. Tremors of the demolition of the Babri Masjid in Ayodhya on 6 December 1992 had caused violent aftershocks in the city, leading to politically-motivated and planned rioting between Hindus and Muslims.

The riots had led to the systematic slaughtering of people from both communities. Several hundreds were killed and thousands rendered homeless by rampaging, angry mobs. Mumbai was literally burning in the fire of religious discord.

Specific Muslim locations like Bhendi Bazaar, Dongri,

Nagpada, Dharavi and Mumbra had become epicentres for all the wrong things that occurred in the city. Labelled as 'sensitive zones', these areas saw tremendous bloodshed and destruction.

The army, unable to control the riots, was forced to declare curfew.

Amidst all this, an old, fragile-looking, seventy-two-year-old had alone taken the lead in bringing peace back to Dongri. All her power centres in the underworld were fading fast. Top mafia bosses Karim Lala and Mastan were old and ailing, and living a retired existence, while Vardha had long since died after retreating to Chennai in 1988. Reigning ganglord Dawood had also relocated to Dubai. And so, as far as wielding power was concerned, she was left with nothing.

The incidents over the past few days had pained her. Several people had approached her for help. They had cried about the loss of property, the burning down of their houses and the brutal killing of their sons and families. They begged for help and she was trying her best, too. She had called the police, ganglords, politicians, but they all confessed that the situation had gone way beyond the control of ordinary men.

It had been a month since the riots had first started and she could see how law enforcement bodies had failed to quell the growing turmoil in the city. Now, all that she could do to console these anxious souls was to ask them to look for answers in prayer. The only window and door in her room had been locked for days and heavy curtains shielded from her all that was happening outside.

Earlier, a reprimand from her window would have silenced any sort of violent activity below. Today, however, no one cared. She had seen thousands gather to protest the demolition of the Babri Masjid and had also noticed how the mob turned violent and set police vehicles on fire. She requested them to stop but no one heeded her.

Her power had been mutilated with the Hindu-Muslim riots. She had been asked to stay put. But, for how long ... she wondered.

The Suleman Usman Bakery firing on 9 January 1993, however, was the last straw for her. The Special Operation Squad (SOS), suspecting terrorists were holed up on the terrace of Suleman Usman Bakery, had—under the direction of joint commissioner of police R.D. Tyagi—opened fire inside the bakery. She had peered through her windows and heard the gunshots and helpless cries of people from inside the bakery; she was spectator to one of the most gruesome and unwarranted killings by the police.

The firing had resulted in the death of nine Muslims. But the police failed to apprehend terrorists or seize firearms from the spot; the truth being that there were neither.

Now, even a hundred warnings by the forces would not shake her determination to step out of her home. In her long white chikan nightgown and a shawl that covered the grey in her hair, this fair and heavily jewelled lady, with a rosary in one hand and a white flag in the other, went out onto the street. In a few seconds, a group of young men had gathered behind her as she led the demonstration.

She walked between the torched lanes of Dongri towards the Pydhonie junction, unconcerned about danger.

The junction with the Hamidiya Masjid on the right, Khatri Masjid on the left and three Jain Derasars, had become the dividing line for the two wounded communities. The Pydhonie police station, a gift of the British era, stood at right angles from these religious houses. When she reached the junction, she stopped.

Here she stood, flanked by hundreds of young men and women, waving her flag and screaming for peace and harmony even as injured bodies lay strewn and mobs openly ransacked shops in the vicinity, setting them on fire.

On seeing the demonstrating crowd, the police with their lathis and shields began closing in towards them. Her tired old legs had given in, but Jenabai stood calm, unafraid of the mob fury and the police lathis. From behind her supporters screamed loudly, 'Jenabai zindabad! Jenabai zindabad! Jenabai zindabad!'

Chapter 12

JENABAI'S DAUGHTER SPEAKS

After days of endless calls and many dead ends, we finally manage to get our hands on the phone number of Jenabai's eldest daughter, Khatum, who is also known as Khadija.

The seventy-four-year-old is extremely cordial on the phone and makes no attempt to hide her happiness when she hears that we are writing about her mother. Even before we know it, we have been invited to her maternal home at the Chunawala building in Dongri.

It is the same house where Jenabai breathed her last, some fourteen years ago. Her daughter now lives here alone after having separated from her husband, who left her for another woman.

The building is considerably old and has only three floors. The entrance leads to a narrow and steep flight of wooden stairs, up which we walk to the first floor. Khadija's room is the second to the right and the door, painted a pale white, is protected by iron grills. After we ring the bell twice, a tall woman opens the door. She is wearing a long, pale pink salwar-kameez, and her head is covered with a dupatta.

With a smile, she allows us in. 'Too many robbers,' she says, as she fumbles with the iron grill to close it again. She introduces herself as Khadija and offers us a seat on her small sofa. The marble-tiled room is not big, and even without concrete walls, the 150-square-foot room evidently serves as drawing room, bedroom, kitchen and balcony.

The sofa that we sit on faces a bed, above which a large picture of the Holy Kaaba in Mecca crafted on cloth hangs on the wall. Khadija sits on the bed facing us.

She is broad-shouldered and over 5' 11 in height. Her large, gaunt nose is very much like her mother's.

She sheds a little more light on Jenabai for us. 'Powerful, fearless and abusive—these are three words that best describe my mother. She was a typical godmother, and for a long time this home of hers was the ground to settle thousands of family disputes, and endless battles within the mafia.'

Khadija doesn't really know when her mother gained this godmother-like stature. But, 'She would sit on this same bed and give solutions to those who lined up outside our house with their problems. Our home was always bustling with people,' she confirms.

Khadija also speaks of how her mother had tried to get her into becoming an informer. She accepts that she lacked the charisma and shrewdness of her mother, when it came to dealing with the police. 'I remember her taking me along during one of her rounds of the police station, but I was extremely scared of the uniform-wallahs and told her to keep me away from all this.'

All of a sudden, Khadija gets up from her bed as if remembering something. She moves towards the steel cupboard, opens it and carefully takes out a rosary. 'This is her tasbeeh,' she says, adding, 'it was inseparable from her. She took it everywhere she went.' The death of her son Kamaal and her own ailing health made Jenabai turn to religion. In the late 1980s, she had involved herself in the Tabligh-i-Jamaat, a religious movement among Muslims.

Her death took the family by surprise. Jenabai, in the seventy-four years of her life, had never fallen seriously ill. It was fortunate that she hadn't, because she made her aversion to doctors, medicines and hospitals very obvious.

One day, she had fallen unconscious while praying. 'We rushed her to the hospital,' Khadija says. The doctors diagnosed brain haemorrhage and admitted her in the ICU. 'However, when she gained consciousness and found herself in a hospital, she started screaming and abusing us for bringing her there. She demanded to be taken back home. Since we were all scared of her, we relented.'

Back home, she slipped into a coma. Medical facilities

were provided to her at home itself; however, a week later, she died.

Thus, Zainab Darwesh Gandhi alias Jenabai Daaruwali, died a silent and painless death. All that is left of her now is the carvings on the headstone of her grave: Form no 2544, Otta no 601.

TWO

THE MATRIARCH OF KAMATHIPURA

Chapter 1

THE BIRTH OF A SEX WORKER

She was forced to wear a red, bridal dress and sit on a bed sprinkled liberally with rose petals. Her lips were coloured a blood-red and a huge nose ring adorned her nose, adding to the garishness of her appearance. An old song played again and again on an old gramophone in the room. The setting reminded her of a wedding night; Madhu was still clueless about why she was here.

Suddenly, the door pushed open. A terrified Madhu nearly jumped out of her skin when she saw Jaggan seth enter the room. His eyes were bloodshot—an indication that he had already been drinking heavily—as he looked at the young girl on the bed. In his mind he had visualised the perfect female form, and it matched hers to a tee. He was pleased that he would be the first to have all of her.

Under his gaze, Madhu, though fully clad, felt naked. The sixteen-year-old had no idea that this was her 'nath utaarna' ceremony, a euphemism for what is actually the deflowering of a virgin. The ceremony derives its name from the traditional wedding night, where the husband takes off the golden nose ring (nath) of his virgin bride while making love to her. Among sex workers, however, the nath utaarna is the adolescent's initiation into the sex trade.

Jaggan seth began to take off his clothes and a chill ran down Madhu's spine. She wanted to cry but Madam Rashmi had warned her against crying or showing any sort of reluctance. 'If you cry, that man will thrash you to death. Do as he tells you,' she had said. It was to Madam Rashmi that she had been brought by the men who had kidnapped her from the lodge. Just three weeks ago she had eloped with a man, Shravan, to Mumbai, from her village. They had stayed in a lodge for a few days. One day, some people had come and kidnapped her. Madhu was yet to learn that it was Shravan who had played middleman in selling her off to a brothel for a thousand rupees.

Before she knew what was happening, Jaggan seth had undressed and was sitting down on the bed next to her. A horrible smell—a strange combination of paan, bidis and country liquor—hit her. Madhu turned her head away, unable to breathe properly. There was an odd moment of silence, after which the seth caught her by the arm and whispered in her ear, 'Look at me ...'

Madhu did not respond. Annoyed, the seth took hold of her chin and turned her face towards him. She was forced to look at his naked body. The man was the size of a blimp and had a massive, protruding belly—she was amazed that he felt no shame. Embarrassed, she put her head down.

Jaggan seth pushed her down onto the bed and climbed on top of her. He lifted her ghagra and slid his fingers between her legs, moving them slowly and repeatedly as if to elicit some response. Madhu was shocked; she closed her eyes to say a small prayer, hoping he would stop, not realising that her agony had only just begun. In less than a few minutes, Jaggan seth had stripped her of her red ghagra choli. Madhu tried to resist, but the sixteen-year-old was no match for the obese seth.

Tears rolled down Madhu's cheeks; the more she tried to push him off, the more like an animal he behaved. By the time the seth was done with her—raping her several times, and thrashing her when she tried to hurt him by squeezing his penis too hard—Madhu, shivering, heavily bruised, humiliated, was in so much pain that for the first time since she had run away from home, she began to think of death.

When Rashmi and her husband found out that she had tried to hurt Jaggan seth, they beat up Madhu. They also told her it was Shravan who had sold her to them. And though this came as a shock to her, Madhu did not shed a single tear.

She refused to eat or drink and did not acknowledge the presence of people around her. She had become a stone—as good as dead. Initially, Madam Rashmi forced another man on her but he stormed out angrily in few minutes and demanded his money back, accusing Madam Rashmi of keeping frigid women in her brothel. Fearing a drop in her clients, she decided against sending anyone to Madhu for some time until the girl fully recovered.

However, after a week of sheltering the girl, Rashmi decided that she had had enough. There were only two solutions that she could think of: one was to once again attempt to convince Madhu to accept her lot, and the second was to throw her out. The latter seemed easier but could get her into trouble with the cops. Then she thought of someone, the only person really, who could possibly help her with her dilemma—Gangubai.

Gangubai was a renowned brothel madam in the area. Apart from owning several brothels, she also had immense influence on the women who worked in them. After hearing of Madhu's obduracy, Gangubai decided to come and speak to her. This was a routine job for her and Madhu's behaviour came as no surprise to her.

A five-foot-tall Gangubai, dressed in a white saree, got out of her car and climbed the steps leading to Madhu's room. Other sex workers, who were either peering out of their balconies or were on the road looking for customers, bowed in respect when they saw her enter the building.

Gangubai entered Madhu's room and latched the door; she had ordered everyone to give her some privacy. A chair had specially been placed in the hundred-square-foot room for Gangubai. In a corner of the room was a small cot, where Madhu was sitting cross-legged. Gangubai ignored the chair and went and sat beside her.

'What is your name?' she asked.

There was no response. Madhu had buried her face in her hands and wouldn't look up. Gangubai took hold of her face and forced Madhu to look at her. The girl's eyes were red and puffy from the endless crying. Aware that Madhu needed to be handled carefully, Gangubai took some water from a jug that was on a nearby table and soaked the pallu of her saree in it. Then she delicately wiped Madhu's face with it. Gangubai continued this for a minute or two, until the girl finally broke into tears and hugged Gangubai tightly.

'Please let me go ... please, I beg of you ... otherwise I will die,' she howled.

'I don't speak to people who cry. Look at your state. First stop crying and then I will listen to you. I am here to help you,' Gangubai said.

Madhu forced herself to stop crying.

'What is your name?'

'Madhu ...'

'Madhu beti, why are you behaving like this? You haven't eaten food for so many days. Do you want to kill yourself?' Gangubai asked in a maternal tone.

'I'd rather die than live here.'

'Beti, if you did not want to come here, then how did you land up here in the first place?' Gangubai had not been told about the circumstances under which Madhu had been brought to the brothel.

'Shh … Shravan,' Madhu hesitantly said his name and again broke into tears, the depth of his betrayal overcoming her.

'We ran away from our village in Ratnagiri. He promised to marry me as my parents were against our relationship. But … but they told me that he sold me off to this place. Please … I want to go back home …'

Gangubai was silent; the girl's words had brought back a flood of memories, which took her back to when she was sixteen.

Ganga Harjeevandas Kathiawadi was brought up in the village of Kathiawad in Gujarat. Her family comprised reputed lawyers and educationists, and shared strong ties with the royal Kathiawadi family. Ganga's father and brothers were strict disciplinarians and took a keen interest in her education, unusual for rural families in the 1940s. However, young Ganga's heart lay elsewhere: she was captivated by films and acting. Friends in school who had visited the city of Mumbai spoke to her about its buildings, the cars, the men and the movies, and soon she became obsessed with the desire to visit the place.

This desire only heightened when her father employed twenty-eight-year-old Ramnik Laal as the new accountant. Apart from being besotted by him, Ganga also learned that Ramnik had spent a few years in Mumbai. She found herself drawn to him and began looking for excuses to chat with him. She would visit him on the pretext of offering him tea and lunch in the small room in the corner of her bungalow, and Ramnik did not seem to mind sparing a few minutes of his time for her.

Initially, their discussions were limited to Mumbai and her dreams of becoming an actress, but it soon catapulted into love. Now, Ramnik began meeting Ganga outside school and in the village fields. He promised to get her a role in a film in Mumbai through his contacts in the industry, and then asked if she wanted to marry him. Ganga was ecstatic. She knew that she was treading uncertain ground but for the first time, she was willing to take a risk because she was madly in love with him. However, she knew her parents wouldn't allow her to get married to Ramnik or approve of her choice of career, both of which she wanted desperately. This was when Ramnik asked her to go with him to Mumbai. Ganga immediately accepted the suggestion but her conservative upbringing prevented her from doing so without them getting married first. Hence, the day before they left for Mumbai, Ganga and Ramnik secretly got married at a small temple in Kathiawad. Then she packed a few dresses, cash and her mother's jewellery, on Ramnik's insistence, inside a small cloth bag and they took a train to Mumbai via Ahmedabad. She did not leave any letter and hadn't even told friends about her affair with Ramnik. Once she left, she knew that she could never return to Kathiawad, in order to protect her father's reputation.

Two days later, Ganga and Ramnik got down onto the platform of Bombay Central station. The station was huge and immediately captured Ganga's imagination. She had heard of this place from her friends in school and she was upset that she would no longer be able to share her own tales with them. 'Don't worry, you will make many new friends here. And when your friends from Kathiawad hear about you becoming a big star in Mumbai, they will come here to meet you,' Ramnik assured a teary Ganga.

The couple stayed in a lodge where they made love for the very first time. The next few days were spent roaming around the city. They travelled on trams, local trains, carts and saw the entire city—all with the money Ganga had stolen from her parents' locker. For Ganga, this was all magical and dream-like; she felt no remorse at having left home.

A week later, Ramnik suggested that she stay with his aunt until they found a permanent room. 'The lodge is becoming expensive ... I am going to search for a small room on rent, until then you can stay with my maasi,' he said.

Ganga was surprised because Ramnik had always maintained that he had no relatives in the city; however, she agreed without making too much fuss. Ramnik's aunt came to collect her from the lodge. The woman, who introduced herself as Sheela, did not make a good impression on Ganga. She was garishly dressed and always seemed to be chewing paan. Ramnik hailed a cab for them and made Ganga sit inside, with the promise of returning in a day.

When they turned into the lane that housed Sheela

maasi's home, Ganga drew back in shock at the sight of many half-naked women walking around and peering over balconies. Sheela maasi, sensing Ganga's discomfort, said, 'Women dress differently in different areas of Mumbai.'

'Which area is this?' Ganga asked.

'Kamathipura. Have you heard of it?' Sheela maasi asked.

'No.'

'Good ... this is where I stay. You will be staying here for a while, too,' she said with a smile.

'No, I am here just for a day ...' Ganga said immediately, trying to assure herself.

Sheela maasi chose not to reply, instead turning her head towards the window.

When she got down from the cab, she saw curious eyes on her. Everyone in the area seemed to know Ramnik's maasi; Ganga tried to stay calm, yet Ramnik's absence worried her.

Sheela maasi took her into a small room and asked Ganga to unpack and freshen up.

'I don't need to unpack. I am going tomorrow,' Ganga said.

Sheela maasi looked at her, and then finally said, 'I can't hide this from you any longer. I am not Ramnik's maasi, I run a brothel.'

There was a stinging moment of silence. Ganga was stunned that Ramnik had lied, but the enormity of the situation hadn't yet sunk in. 'Why am I here?' she asked.

'Ramnik sold you to us for five hundred rupees. He won't be coming back; he has gone to Kathiawad.'

'You are lying,' Ganga screamed. She couldn't believe Ramnik, her companion, the person she had trusted completely, had duped her.

'What will I achieve by lying, Ganga? I know you are from a good family but it is your husband who has sold you to us.'

'Why would Ramnik do something like this to me?' she asked.

'I don't know—but now, you will have to listen to us.'

'I won't,' Ganga said angrily and made an attempt to leave the room. But Sheela used all her strength and pulled her back inside.

'Don't take advantage of my goodness! You are in a brothel now and you are here to satisfy my clients. Don't you dare try and run,' Sheela said before walking out of the room and bolting it from the outside.

Days passed; Ganga was beaten and starved because she spent all day crying. Ramnik was still nowhere to be seen and Ganga did not know whether to accept her fate or go home. She had already dishonoured her parents by eloping with Ramnik. Her father, who must have already become a subject of ridicule, would never accept her back. Further, she had other sisters in line for marriage; her family wouldn't risk their futures for Ganga.

Sheela also kept reminding her that, once the villagers of Kathiawad learnt that she had stayed at Kamathipura in Mumbai, they would ostracise her family. Mortified by the likely consequences, Ganga finally decided not to return home.

The only other option left was death, which was almost impossible considering the number of people who kept an eye on her. Two weeks later, Ganga finally gave in. In any case, she thought, her body had already been violated and used by a conman, and there was no way she could erase those scars.

Ganga called for Sheela and told her that she was ready to do whatever she wanted. An excited Sheela hugged her and assured her that the brothel would always take care of her.

That very night, Ganga was sent for her own nath utaarna ceremony. Ramnik had not only lied to Ganga but also to Sheela. He had sold Ganga saying that she was still a virgin, and since Ganga was unaware of the rituals of the sex trade, she didn't reveal this to Sheela.

Ganga went through the nath utarna ceremony stoically. Deep down she cringed but cooperated fully with the seth, knowing that this was now her profession. To her luck, the seth was more than happy with her. After he had finished with her, he tipped her well and also gifted her a gold ring.

On his way out, he had turned around and asked, 'By the way what is your name?'

For a moment she hesitated, and then replied, 'Gangu.' She had decided to do away with everything from her past. From that point on, Ganga became Gangu.

Chapter 2

THE PERVERTED PATHAN

Gangu quickly became one of the most sought-after and well-paid commercial sex workers in Kamathipura. She shut away Kathiawad, Ramnik and everything associated with her past, refusing to think about that part of her life. Seths from as far as Hyderabad, Kolkata and New Delhi specifically asked for her when they were in town. This came as no surprise to Sheela because although Gangu wasn't the most attractive girl in her brothel, men spoke endlessly about her skills in bed.

Gangu had also learned the knack of getting her clients to open their purse strings without getting emotionally involved with any of them. With the money she earned, Gangu would make gold jewellery for herself. This was her only indulgence, apart from the movies that she watched once in a while at a nearby cinema hall. A career in celluloid was now a distant dream for Gangu, but her craze for the movies hadn't diminished. Sheela was aware of her indulgences but was tolerant because she was nervous about losing her cash cow.

When Gangu was twenty-eight, a rowdy Pathan who had heard about the Kathiawadi from other men, barged into Sheela's brothel one day, asking for Gangu. He was over six feet tall and massive compared to the usual clientele. Sheela was hesitant about letting him in to see Gangu but the man's intimidating nature stopped her from saying anything. She reluctantly agreed, hoping that Gangu would put her expertise to good use and tactfully handle this uncouth client. However, the outcome was very different. The Pathan was very brutal with Gangu—she had never experienced such cruelty in bed; and then, he walked out of the brothel without paying Sheela as much as a paisa.

Everyone in the brothel was shocked but no one, including Sheela, complained, fearing that he was connected to a dangerous group of Pathan gangsters in the area. The encounter incapacitated Gangu for over four days, leaving her in no state to entertain her clients. A distressed Sheela apologised to Gangu and told her that she'd ensure that this would never happen to her again.

A month later, the Pathan returned, and this time he was very drunk. When Sheela saw him, she called for two men. However, they were no match for the Pathan, only serving to enrage him further. He stormed into Gangu's room. She was with another client at the time, but the

Pathan threw the man out naked and latched the door. Sheela grew frantic, helplessly banging on the door; she knew that she couldn't involve the cops. This time when he left, the Pathan ensured that Gangu's body was bruised and bitten all over.

After the ordeal, Gangu had to be hospitalised and was forced to lie in her room like an invalid for weeks. Gangu was not only angry with herself for her helplessness but also with Sheela, when she learned that Sheela hadn't done anything to solve her problem.

After having a bitter argument with Sheela, Gangu finally took it upon herself to deal with the Pathan. Gangu realised that if she remained quiet now, it would set a precedent for bigger problems in the future. She began making enquiries about the man. Finally, through one of her clients, she learnt that he was called Shaukat Khan and was associated with the Karim Lala gang.

Abdul Karim Khan, known as Karim Lala, was still a small-time gangster at the time. He was known for being respectful towards women. In those days, he headed a Pathan organisation called the Pakhtoon Jirgai Hind. Gangu felt that if anything had to be done, it would have to be through Karim Lala. The other girls, including Sheela, tried to dissuade her from meeting him because he was infamous for his activities and aggressiveness in south Mumbai, but she remained obstinate.

One Friday afternoon, when Karim Lala had just finished offering his Jumma namaaz and was walking towards his home at Tahir Manzil in Lamington Road, Gangu accosted him. She had been waiting outside Baida Galli, the lane that led to his home.

'Karim bhai, salaam. I need a small favour from you,' she said.

From her appearance, the dour Pathan figured that she was a commercial sex worker from the nearby area.

'What is it about?' he demanded, taken aback by her boldness and uncomfortable about talking to a sex worker on the road.

'It is about one of your men.'

Surprised, he said, 'Come home, we will talk there. It doesn't seem right to talk here,' he said and marched down the lane, with Gangu following him.

Karim Lala was averse to entertaining a sex worker in his house, and so he asked her to head towards his building's terrace while he changed into his home clothes. Tea and snacks were sent up for her. Ten minutes later, when Karim Lala went up to his terrace, he noticed that Gangu hadn't touched anything that had been served to her.

'Why haven't you eaten?'

'If you have a problem with a person of my reputation stepping inside your home, then it would be wrong for me to dirty the crockery that comes from the kitchen of your house.'

Karim Lala was speechless.

'What is your name?' he asked finally.

'Gangu ... I work in Kamathipura.'

'What do you want from me?'

'Bhai, I don't know if you ever see faults in your own men and have ever punished them, especially if they have done something wrong to a person like me. But if you do, I am ready to serve you as your concubine for life,' she said.

Karim Lala's face grew red; nobody had ever dared to talk to him like this. Yet he tried to stay calm and said, 'I am a family man, so don't ever make such an offer to me again. And concerning my men, if they have erred I'm ready to pull them up. But who is the person?'

'Shaukat Khan. I have heard that he is in your gang.'

'My gang ... I don't know of any such man.'

'I've made enquiries ...'

'Hmm ... What has he done?'

'He raped me twice in the last few weeks and hasn't paid me for the services. I might be a prostitute but I am not an object that people can use whenever they feel like. Because of that man, I had to be hospitalised ... he was very brutal to me ...' Gangu said and showed him the scars on her hands and arms.

The scars were so horrific that Karim Lala actually put his head down. He was aghast at the cruelty that had been inflicted on her, that too by a Pathan who allegedly belonged to his group.

'Gangu, the next time he comes to you, I want a message to be delivered to me. Keep him busy until I come. I will personally deal with him. Now you can go.'

Gangu smiled and removed a small thread from her purse. 'Karim bhai, it has been years since I tied a rakhi for anyone because ever since I was brought here, I never felt safe with any man. Today, by offering me protection, you have only reinstilled my faith in brotherhood.'

The Pathan ganglord was amazed at Gangu's impudence. A young woman, who just a few minutes ago had said that she was ready to be his mistress, was now telling him she wanted to make him her brother. He smiled and brought his hand forward and allowed her to tie the thread, saying, 'You have my word on this. From now on you are my sister.'

Then he took a sweet from the snacks on the plate and fed her. 'I hope you won't complain now,' he said. Gangu was elated.

Karim Lala planted a mole right outside Sheela's brothel in Kamathipura; this young man kept a check on all the customers who visited Gangu on a daily basis. For days together, there was no sign of Shaukat Khan; Gangu was disappointed—she hoped he would come so Karim Lala could put him in his place.

It was three weeks before he came to the brothel again. Gangu sent a message through another sex worker to the mole, who in turn rushed to Karim Lala's house on his cycle. Khan was more aggressive and vicious this time but Gangu decided to fully cooperate until Karim Lala came on the scene. In less than ten minutes, she heard a loud thumping on the door. 'Open the door!'

The voice, though unfamiliar, had an ominous tone to it. Angry at another attempt to stall him in the brothel, Khan slapped Gangu and got up. Little did he realise that he would be confronted by none other than Karim Lala himself. Gangu rushed to cover herself with a sheet.

Shaukat Khan's jaw dropped when he saw Lala and two other Pathans at the door with hockey sticks in their hands. He hurriedly put on his trousers and was looking for an escape, when Karim Lala dragged him out of the brothel. Then he started beating Khan up mercilessly with the hockey stick. Khan tried to stop him and also spoke to him in desperation in Pashtoon, accusing Karim Lala of going against his own race for a whore. This further angered Karim Lala, who kicked him hard in his stomach and knocked Khan on the head with the stick. 'Don't you dare call yourself a Pathan!' Karim Lala thundered.

Finally, when Karim Lala was satisfied that he had broken enough bones to render Khan an invalid for weeks, he stopped. 'Gangu is my rakhi sister. The next time anyone treats her badly, I will kill them,' he announced loudly, warning everyone in Kamathipura.

From then on, things changed for Gangu. People in Kamathipura now started treating her differently. Her connection with the most feared gangster in south Mumbai put her on another pedestal altogether. Nobody, not even Sheela, dared to take advantage of her. An entirely new world opened up to Gangu. Under the tutelage of her rakhi brother, she began to develop strong ties with the Nagpada police and the underworld.

When Sheela suddenly passed away some time later, people coaxed Gangu to stand for the customary local gharwali elections.* She immediately agreed, hoping that this would put paid to her job as a prostitute. It came as no surprise when she won the election and went on to become a brothel madam at a very young age.

Gangu was now called Gangubai Kathewali, a distorted version of the word kothewali, which also means 'performing sex workers'. Gangubai chose to call herself Kathewali, a last remaining association with her family name, Kathiawadi.

* Brothel keepers are usually referred to as gharwalis. Red-light areas have their own hierarchy, and sex workers rise in stature if they win an election. A gharwali usually runs a certain number of pinjras (cages or compact beds) under her command.

Chapter 3

THE PROTECTOR

Gangubai Kathewali was brought back to the present by the sound of Madhu's wailing. 'Will you stop crying? People will think I'm torturing you,' Gangubai said impatiently.

'Please get me out of here,' Madhu cried again.

The old woman placed her hand on Madhu's cheek and said, 'Okay, just for a moment assume that I have allowed you to go ... what will you do after that?'

'I will go back to my village in Ratnagiri,' Madhu replied immediately.

'To whom?'

'What kind of question is this? Of course, to my parents,' the girl said.

'Aye ladki, don't you dare back-answer ...' Gangubai warned.

The sixteen-year-old immediately apologised. Gangubai ignored her apology and continued. 'You do realise that you have brought a lot of shame to your parents after eloping with your lover. If the people in your village find out that you were in Kamathipura, you will be an outcast.'

'My parents might accept me if I don't tell them about this place.' Madhu retorted.

'What will you tell them then?' she asked, surprised by the girl's confidence.

'I don't know ...'

There was a long pause, following which Gangubai said, 'Like you, even I had run away. I was your age when my husband sold me off ... I never returned because if my family learnt that I had come from Kamathipura, they would have killed me. There was no option but to make this place my home. And even if you do return to your family, what's to stop them from ostracising you? There was a girl here, Vinita, who thought her family was different and went back to them.' Gangubai was quiet for a few seconds before she said, 'We heard a few months later from one of the boys in her village that she was the victim of an honour killing.'

Madhu began weeping again. 'Does that mean I have to stay here forever?' she asked.

'I didn't say that. I just want to know if you will be able to convince your parents.'

'I can at least try,' Madhu said, adding, 'I realise I have wronged, and I have already paid the price for this. Just give me one opportunity to ask for forgiveness; if I fail, I will take up a small job in Ratnagiri but I don't want to live here.'

Gangubai looked at Madhu's face, as if trying to read her mind. After a few minutes she got up, opened the door and called out for Madam Rashmi.

'Let her go,' Gangubai told Madam Rashmi when she entered, 'she is not meant to stay here.' Madam Rashmi was shocked. 'But we have paid a thousand rupees for her. How can we let her go?'

'I am aware of that. You can attribute it to business loss. In future, I don't want any girl being pushed around against her will. Do you understand?' Gangubai asked. 'Just ensure that she is put on the right bus for Ratnagiri. If possible, send Pappu to drop her.' Saying this Gangubai left the room, leaving no opportunity for Madhu to thank her.

The news of Gangubai's gesture spread like wildfire through the narrow lanes of Kamathipura. She was now known as the only brothel madam who did not give priority to business and money but to women. Madhu's flight also set a precedent for several other women, who now approached Gangubai. If their cases were genuine, Gangubai allowed them to leave; if not, she ensured that their escape was improbable. She had come to control Kamathipura's brothels with an iron fist and her popularity among the people there soared with time. She protected the sex workers from men like Shaukat Khan who either abused the women or took advantage of them by promising them marriage or did not pay them for sex. These men feared Gangubai for her connections with the underworld and the police; the sex workers, on the other hand, revered her as a mother, calling her Ganguma. Her victory in the bade* gharwali elections only strengthened this position.

Gangubai openly advocated the need for prostitution belts in cities. She is still remembered for a speech she gave during a women's conference at Azad Maidan. A meeting had been called in support of the girl child and empowerment of women. Women from several leading political parties, NGOs and other organisations had been called. Gangubai, too, had been invited to extend help in promoting literacy among prostitutes. The organisers had asked her to speak on the condition of women in brothels. However, when she was called to the podium and introduced as the 'president of Kamathipura', she was greeted with a lot of suspicion. Gangubai, dressed in a white cotton saree, sensed their animosity. Gangubai had been nervous when she ascended the stairs to the podium—she had never really spoken in public before this. She had rehearsed her speech several times during the day, yet standing there in front of such a large crowd, she felt absolutely unprepared. Even as she came closer to the microphone, she could hear murmurings among a section

* The gharwali elections is followed by the bade gharwali elections. While the gharwali usually has an entire floor to herself with forty pinjras or more, the bade gharwali has an entire building under her jurisdiction. Every bade gharwali has a few gharwalis reporting to her. The command was thus decentralised and Gangubai was at the helm of this structure for over sixteen years.

of the crowd. But the crowd's behaviour only made her more determined to prove her point and all of a sudden, she became less nervous.

Gangubai stunned her organisers and the audience with the opening line of her speech: 'I am a gharwali (a brothel madam) not a ghar todnewali (home wrecker). Several people among you look at this title as a stigma on womanhood but it is this stigma that has saved the chastity, integrity and morality of several thousands of women.'

The crowd grew silent. Gangubai continued, 'Unlike other cities of India, the streets of Mumbai are far safer today. You will rarely hear of an incident where a girl is sexually assaulted on the roads. I don't want to take away any credit from the city's administration but I also firmly believe that the notorious women of Kamathipura should be partly credited for this.

'We are only second to the legitimately married gharwalis (housewives). By giving ourselves to the carnal pursuits of men, we are doing a big favour to all the women in society. A few handful of women who cater to the physical needs of men are actually protecting all of you from being attacked. These women help blunt the bestial male aggression, which is something that cannot be done in my hometown in Gujarat,' she said. 'You might think that we enjoy doing what we do. Believe me, it is not easy for us. Most of us are forced to do this because we have families to look after. It shames me to learn that society looks down upon its very protectors. Just like the jawans of our country, who fight endlessly in the battlefield so that you remain unharmed, we prostitutes too, are fighting our own battles every day. Then why the difference? Why is a jawan rewarded and given national honours, while prostitutes are insulted and treated like pariahs? Give me an answer.'

The crowd listened to Gangubai with rapt attention. Gangubai, on the other hand, seemed like she was in a trance, overpowered by very strong emotions, 'Nobody will have an answer,' she said, 'because you all are responsible for creating this question in the first place. The only solution to the problem is by treating sex workers as equals. The day you manage to do this, I will believe that society has achieved "women empowerment". If an orthodox city like Hyderabad can name its red-light area Mehboob ki Mehndi (the henna of the beloved), why does "Kamathipura" draw expressions of disgust in this so- called "forward-looking" city of Bombay? Before I end, I would like to draw one last parallel. We all keep at least one toilet in our homes so that we do not defecate or urinate in other rooms. This is the same reason why there is a need for a prostitution belt in each and every city. I'd like to make a humble plea to the government to allow red- light areas to co-exist in society.'

The crowd was immediately on its feet and applauding thunderously. Nobody had ever spoken for the cause of sex workers so convincingly.

Chapter 4

A MOTHER MALIGNED

Gangubai's speech was reported widely in several regional newspapers and she rose suddenly to stardom. Several ministers and journalists visited her, impressed by her courage in fighting the system and trying to decriminalise prostitution. She now surfaced as a force in society in her own right.

In the 1950s and '60s, commercial sex workers occupied the western strip of Kamathipura between Suklaji Street, Manaji Rauji Street and part of Foras Road from Alexandria Cinema up to the point where it met Jairaj Bhai Lane. At the time, sex workers did not cross Manaji Rauji Street or pass through the central and eastern areas of Kamathipura as people in the area did not like it. However, children attending the municipal school at the junction of Kamathipura 7th Street and people visiting the several temples located in the west of Kamathipura had to pass through the brothel areas. Further, St Anthony's Girls' High School, built in the early 1920s, had its entrance from Bellasis Road. The school building at the rear overlooked Kamathipura 14th Street, which was then inhabited by over 250 sex workers, who could also be seen from the upper floor of the building.

Early in the year 1960, authorities of the St Anthony's Girls' High School as well as locals living in the vicinity of Kamathipura, wanted part of the red-light belt evacuated because they felt that sex workers could have a negative influence on the minds of young students. The school authorities cited that prostitution could not be carried out within two hundred yards from an educational institution. A strong movement picked up against the presence of the red-light zone. There were constant agitations and meetings with the civic authorities; but both parties refused to budge from their position.

When the anti-prostitution sentiment swelled, sex workers sought Gangubai's help and she successfully spearheaded the movement against the evacuation of sex workers from the belt.

Her political connections apparently also won her an appointment with the then prime minister of India, Jawaharlal Nehru, at his residence in New Delhi. Once again, Gangubai made history by becoming the only local brothel madam to secure an appointment with the head of the country.

Not much is known about the last years of Gangubai

Kathewali. Most people remember her for her gold-bordered white sarees and gold-buttoned blouses. Gangubai loved flaunting her collection of gold jewellery. She also wore gold-rimmed glasses and had an artificial gold tooth. She was also the only brothel keeper of her time to own a black Bentley car. However, it is still not known how she managed to accumulate so much wealth in her lifetime.

While she never got married, she is said to have adopted several children who lived with her in her small room in Kamathipura 12th Lane. Most of them were either orphans or homeless. Gangubai took a keen interest in bringing them up and ensured they received a good education. Of all these children, only one, Babbi, lives in Kamathipura today.

A social worker from the area who was initially sheltered by Gangubai, describes her as 'the queen of Kamathipura'. 'Even today, framed pictures and statuettes of Gangubai are there in the brothels of Kamathipura. Ask anyone about Gangubai and they'll direct you to a framed picture of hers in their room. They may not have known her but they have surely heard of her,' she said.

Gangubai's goodness is, of course, just one side of the coin. A former restaurateur in Kamathipura, puts it aptly. 'It is not like she was all milk and honey. We mustn't forget that she was running a brothel at the end of the day. It is not easy to have thousands of woman working for you ... there was surely a dark side to her that people have chosen to forget. You cannot prosper in this business otherwise.'

According to Babbi, 'Ganguma began her day reading the Gujarati newspaper *Janmbhoomi* and sipping her tea at 6 in the morning. This was followed by breakfast, after which she played cards next door. She was a hard-core gambler and gambled almost daily. She had many vices—she smoked bidis, drank Ranichaap and chewed paan. She also hobnobbed with several journalists and ministers. Gangubai died of old age some time between 1975 and 1978. Soon after, effigies of her were placed in the brothels of the area.

Today, Kamathipura 12th Lane, which was once said to be the richest lane in the area, is a shadow of its former self. In abysmal contrast to its former glory, there is nothing much to see here these days, except for hand-carts, stray dogs or ordinary people engaging in petty work. The lane, which used to be lined with Ambassadors, Mercedes and Bentleys, is now filled with cycles and rusting scooters. Unlike the other by-lanes, 12th Kamathipura has only a brothel or two and it is certainly a far cry from the time of the iron-willed Gangubai.

The canvas of her remarkable life is replete with numerous anecdotes and stories that have now become lore. One of the most legendary Gangubai tales is an apocryphal story, still narrated with pride and great authority by the sex workers of Kamathipura. This incident hasn't been documented or written about, neither is there any existing proof to confirm its authenticity. Its credibility can only be weighed by verbal evidence, as the story seems to have been passed down through word of mouth for over four decades and is one of the few thriving memories of Gangubai. In a private meeting with Pandit Nehru, she explained to him the importance of the red-light area in Mumbai and the need to protect it. Gangubai is also said to have convinced and impressed Nehru with her wit and clarity of thought. During the meeting, Nehru asked her why she had gotten into the business when she could have easily landed herself a good job or husband.

An intrepid Gangubai is said to have thrown a proposal at him. She told him that if he was ready to make her Mrs Nehru, she would be willing to abandon her business for good. Nehru was taken aback, and reprimanded her for having dared to talk to him like that. But a calm Gangubai smiled and said, 'Don't get angry Pradhan Mantriji. I just wanted to prove a point; it is always easier to preach than practise.' Nehru remained silent.

At the end of the meeting, Nehru, who had bluntly rejected her second proposal, conceded to Gangubai's first demand and also promised to look into the matter. Following the intervention of the government, the movement to displace the sex workers died a quick death. Gangubai's argument that the school had been built a century after the prostitution belt had come up, made her a clear winner in the battle. 'Were the concerned authorities blind when they built the school?' she queried.

Gangubai had won the day, thus saving thousands of sex workers from financial desperation, not for the first time in her life.

THREE

FEMME FATALE

PROLOGUE

Ashraf had been feeling uncomfortable since morning. She'd woken up earlier than usual because of a bad dream: she couldn't really remember what she had dreamed, only the vague sense of it being something bad lingered.

Her cup of tea lay cold, untouched, as did the eggs and toast sitting in front of her. She tried to skim through the newspaper but nothing could distract her from the sense of unease she was feeling. She decided to go and meet an old friend and was in her bedroom getting ready, when she heard a loud knock on her front door.

In the past, she had opened her door to all kinds of men: from policemen to thugs holding menacing weapons. Most times, they came with bad news. Today, she wanted to see none of them.

Yet, being the only person at home, she gathered courage and opened the door to find her neighbour, panting, as if he had come running from his house.

'Mehmood bhai has called from Dubai. Come quickly, he said he will call back soon.'

Hearing Mehmood's name, her restive gloom lifted. She put on her chappals quickly and rushed out of the door towards her neighbour's house, leaving her own home unlatched.

She reached their house in less than a minute but had to wait for five minutes before the phone rang again. When it did, she picked up the receiver and was about to say something, when the line on the other end went dead. She put the receiver down and sat quietly in anticipation of another call. It was ten minutes later that the phone rang again. She picked it up. This time, she could clearly hear the person on the other end. He had a husky voice, and since it was an international call, he sounded louder than usual—it was Mehmood. The last time she had heard from him was ten days ago.

'Jaan, I will be back this evening,' he said. 'Please come to the airport ...'

Ashraf was thrilled. Somehow he must have sensed her unease, her anxiety to see him, she thought, despite the distance. After a brief conversation that lasted barely a couple of minutes, he hung up, giving her the flight details. An overwhelming feeling of happiness gripped her. She rushed back to her own house to get ready to meet her husband, Mehmood.

A strikingly attractive young woman, Ashraf had fallen in love with Mehmood when she first met him at a friend's wedding. When, some time later, Mehmood went on to ask her to marry him, she hadn't hesitated for a moment before she said yes. In the five years they'd been together, his one aim had been to make her happy. Ashraf had grown up in a rigid, conservative family and she embraced the freedom that marriage to Mehmood gave her. She travelled with him and lived the life of a queen. Her love for him knew no bounds, and even a brief period of separation hit her hard. The only problem Ashraf had with Mehmood was that she was unsure about what it was he did for a living.

Ashraf did not like the men her husband hobnobbed with and the way they referred to him—his associates called him Mehmood Kalia because of his dark complexion. She took offence at this, and it had added to her dislike of these men. When she complained to Mehmood about what they called him, he affectionately said it was a non- issue. Again, when she conveyed her apprehensions about his working with them, he merely told her not to worry. But he would never explain what his work entailed exactly; what he did, where and with whom he went, was something she was completely ignorant of.

The clock on her dressing-table struck three as Ashraf slipped the last of her gold bangles on her arms. Mehmood would be at the Santa Cruz airport in an hour. She hurriedly picked up her handbag and headed out for the main road at Nagpada. She had already decided to take a cab instead of a train to the airport.

She managed to reach the airport by 4 p.m. People around her were carrying placards, flowers or small gifts to welcome their loved ones. Ashraf looked down at her bare hands and felt guilty. But then she knew that Mehmood was not a materialistic person and that nothing on earth would match up to the happiness he'd feel on seeing her.

She waited patiently, scanning the crowd every time a group of people emerged from the arrival area. She glanced again at the two police jeeps parked right behind her. They'd been there when she'd come, and though she had a faint idea about her husband's poor track record with the cops, today, she tried hard not to read too much into it.

Forty minutes passed but there was still no sign of him. The police jeeps were still parked in the same place but she couldn't see any policemen, so Ashraf didn't feel too concerned.

Finally, a little before five, the sliding doors of the Arrival section opened and she saw a burly, dark man come out along with other people. A black bag hung from his left shoulder. Ashraf broke into a smile and went closer to the railing and tried to catch his attention. His eyes searched for and finally found her in the crowd. Ashraf had just begun to take a few steps towards him when abruptly Mehmood disappeared in a group of men.

Ashraf saw one of the men who had surrounded Mehmood fire two to three gunshots in the air. The Arrival area broke into chaos; people started running helter- skelter in fright and the group of men managed to disappear in the crowd. Ashraf looked for Mehmood in the pandemonium but couldn't spot him. Even as the crowd grew more chaotic, she refused to move, hoping her husband would emerge from the crowd, hold her tight and take her away. Ashraf continued to look for him, when, from within the crowd, she noticed a few men with service revolvers accompanied by cops. Immediately she turned around, only to see that the police jeeps, which had been standing behind her all this while, were missing.

Over the noise of the crowd, she thought she heard faint gunshots from the parking lot. Her heart pounding, she began running towards the parking lot. The car park was a sprawling area but she immediately spotted several policemen huddled together at one end. Just then, one of the jeeps that had earlier been parked behind her, went past her, along with an ambulance, out of the airport. Determined to find out Mehmood's whereabouts, she ran towards the policemen.

When she reached them, she saw a pool of blood near a parked taxi. The cops were preoccupied with drawing white markings on the ground. She froze. She did not know what had happened and how to react. All this while, Ashraf still hoped that Mehmood, who she had seen standing, smiling at her, only five minutes ago, would come and reassure her that he was fine. But there was no sign of him.

She overheard one of the policemen say that the man who had been shot had been taken to Cooper Hospital. Ashraf hailed a taxi and directed it to the hospital. However, when she reached, both the reception and the hospital staff were unaware of any patient who had been admitted with gunshot wounds. They asked Ashraf to instead inquire with the Andheri police station. Ashraf had led a protected life so far; but now she steeled herself and went from station to station in the area, trying to find out where her husband was. Finally, a policeman directed her to J.J. Hospital. At J.J., her worst fears were realised: she was told that a man named Mehmood Khan, a wanted gangster, had been shot dead in an encounter at Santa Cruz airport.

Ashraf knew this was a lie. Mehmood would not have been able to carry a gun past airport security—there was no way he could have been armed. She asked to see the body immediately, with the small hope that perhaps it wasn't her Mehmood, after all, that they were talking about. One of the nurses led her to the morgue. She entered the dimly-lit room and began to tremble when she saw the wrapped bodies. Her legs shook in nervousness; she wished she did not have to witness this all alone. Pitying her, the nurse held Ashraf's hand firmly and took her to a body.

It was him. It was the same man she had seen a few hours ago, the same man who had smiled at her before he'd disappeared into a crowd.

Ashraf bent slightly and held the body in her arms. The last time she had held him this close was the night before he was leaving for Dubai. He had made love to her at that time, passionately. She reached for his lifeless fingers and entwined her own with them. These were the same fingers that had wiped her tears when she was upset.

The vague premonition that had left her anxious earlier

during the day had finally revealed itself. Mehmood was dead. He was gone.

Mehmood's body was buried the next day at Nariawali Qabrastan. Ashraf was not allowed in the burial ground but she stubbornly waited outside the masjid until all the rites were performed.

The previous night, she had been told by hospital staff that her husband had been declared dead on admission. The report had stated that he had died of four bullets in an encounter, after he fired at the cops. The next morning, her relatives had told her that the press had reported that police inspector Emanuel Amolik had led the encounter. She thought about the officer, memorising his name. Preoccupied with her thoughts, she remained unaware that she was being observed by someone who had come to pay his respects to her husband.

The namaaz-e-janaza was read and the body buried. Ashraf watched from far, like a wooden doll, eyes dry but hardened with grief. It was late evening by the time all the necessary rites were completed. When the crowd left, her relatives tried to get her to leave with them. She refused, saying she wanted to be alone for some time. Finally, tired of trying to persuade her, they gave in and left without her. When everyone had gone and it was silent all around, Ashraf quietly slipped into the graveyard. She moved towards the freshly-made grave; once there, she fell to her knees and dug her fingers into the mud. The thought of her husband lying there, below the mud, crippled her.

For the first time since his death, Ashraf cried. She stayed there for a long time, weeping. When the sky had grown dark and the silence was eerie, she decided to leave. She had just begun to lift herself, when an old man came and stood beside her. He held a glass of water in his hand. Discomfited by his presence, Ashraf started straightening her burqa and wiping her tears.

'Drink some water,' he said, handing the glass to her. When Ashraf politely refused, the man remained silent. Ashraf presumed that he was the caretaker and waited for him to reprimand her for entering the graveyard. When he remained quiet, she finally asked him why he was there. This is when he spoke.

'Please accept my condolences. My name is Usmaan and I knew your husband very well. He was a very nice man.' She sighed, thanked him and moved forward to leave the graveyard.

'I know who killed your husband,' the man said suddenly. Ashraf stopped.

'Your husband and I had a common enemy. He doesn't live here. The man who planned his killing is actually someone sitting in Dubai.'

Ashraf was confused: she had been told that an officer had shot her husband; now this old man was talking knowledgeably about someone else being responsible for the murder. She knew that Mehmood had been close to someone in Dubai, and that his recent trip had been to see to some business that needed to be settled urgently.

'Who?' she enquired.

'His name is Dawood,' the old man said. 'Mehmood refused to do some work that Dawood had told him to, which is why Dawood decided to have him killed here. He tipped off the cops about your husband's arrival yesterday.'

Ashraf eyes widened in shock. 'Why did he have to kill my husband? Wasn't there another way to resolve their differences?' she asked, tears slowly beginning to fill her eyes again.

'Dawood wanted to make Mehmood an example for people. He orchestrated the murder so that others wouldn't make the same mistake your husband did.'

Things began to fall in place for Ashraf. In the last month, she had noticed that her husband had not been himself. He had been disturbed. He had also told her that this was going to be his last trip to Dubai as he wanted to settle matters with his boss once and for all. Of all the things she had heard since her husband's death, what this man had just told her was the most believable.

Then the old man said something that set the ground for the change that would occur in Ashraf's life: 'Don't you want to take revenge?'

Ashraf looked at the old man, shocked and confused at the same time. 'What kind of question is this?' she asked in between sobs.

'See, there is no point in crying now. Your husband has gone ... he won't come back. But you need to deal with those who were responsible for this; don't you want them to pay for what they have done?' he asked.

Ashraf immediately replied, 'Of course! That man deserves to die.'

'So, how do you think he will get his punishment?' he asked softly.

'I will complain to the police. I will tell them that they were tricked by that man in Dubai.'

'Oh ...' he smiled, 'and you think that they are going to believe you? Beti, most of these police officers are on Dawood's pay-roll. You won't get anywhere by doing that. In fact they might take you down, just like they killed Mehmood.'

'Then, what do I do?' she asked desperately, still crying.

'Hussain Ustara,' Usmaan said. 'He knows everything about Dawood and hates him. There are not many who would be willing to stand against Dawood and help you but Hussain is a renegade and has his own axe to grind against Dawood. He has a gang of his own and he knows how to use weapons; he might help you. He lives in Pydhonie.'

Ashraf stood quietly for a second or two, then, thanking him, she slowly walked out of the graveyard.

Chapter 1

ON THE TRAIL OF A GUNMAN

After walking past a series of crowded streets, the man finally turns into a filthy, narrow lane. He goes down a couple of metres before stopping in front of a building. He turns to the two men who have been patiently following him all this while. With a grin on his scarred face, he asks them to go up. The men look at each other for a brief second and then, without a word exchanged between them, enter the building and head up a narrow flight of stairs.

The inside of the building has the sense of a dungeon: dark, stale air, and a creepiness about it. The men spot small cameras spying on them as they walk up, but choose not to discuss it. Both are writers by profession: I, then a budding crime reporter, and Vikram Chandra, already an established author after two bestselling novels—*Love and Longing in Bombay* and *Red Earth and Pouring Rain*. He is in the middle of his third, much-awaited book, *Sacred Games*. We've already met the retired, ageing don, Karim

Lala, and the gangster-turned-politician, Arun Gawli. According to the police, neither of these two have used firearms, and Vikram now wants to meet a gangster who has wielded guns.

After a lot of convincing, I have managed to fix an interview with the notorious gangster and police informer Hussain Ustara. When we reach the floor on which we have been told he lives, we see a brown, painted door left ajar. The man who has led us through the confusing alleys of Dongri is now standing behind us; he guides us into the flat.

Vikram sees another camera at the entrance. When he moves the door slightly to enter, he realises that the door is not made of wood, but metal. The security, we realise, is an indication of the current threat to Ustara's life. Ustara has informed on underworld kingpin Dawood Ibrahim on several occasions, and his life now hangs in the balance.

The drawing room is simply furnished, there are only a few pieces of furniture. A man with a small paunch dressed in a white tailored shirt and trousers sits on a couch. I indicate to Vikram, with my eyes, that this is Ustara. Vikram gives a slight nod to indicate that he understands.

There is a table behind Ustara, on which closed circuit television screens rest. Ustara asks us to sit down on the couch that faces him.

'Salaam ... tashrif rakhiye (take a seat).' The atmosphere is relaxed and Vikram and I sit on the couch without any hesitation.

The man's sophistication and flawless Urdu surprise us, given his means of livelihood. He is not the stereotypical Mumbai 'bhai' or 'goonda' and astonishes us even more when he calls for tea and biscuits. He then begins speaking of how he and I have met a few times, and is keen on knowing about Vikram.

When Vikram finishes talking about his book, Ustara asks, 'So how can I help you?'

'I'd like to know everything about your world and its people,' Vikram replies.

Ustara laughs. 'Zaidi can tell you about us. He is a crime reporter.'

'I know, but I still want to hear it from you,' states Vikram.

'Trust me, there is nothing I can say that can interest you. Right now, as you see, I am stranded between life and death. I am just here to do my job like you men.'

Ustara doesn't seem as if he is in a talkative mood, but finally comes around. He speaks to us about his life, his early use of razors ('ustara', thus the name) to settle arguments, and how he rose to command his own gang. Vikram is systematically taking down notes, only interrupting the flow now and then with questions.

However, when Ustara starts speaking about his feud with Dawood Ibrahim, he stops midway, as if a lump has gotten stuck in his throat. Both of us wait for him to speak. He doesn't. I think of diverting the conversation to his personal life.

'What about women?' I ask.

Ustara grins, as if he was just getting there. 'Who doesn't like them?' he says, and then adds, 'but no one could compare with Sapna.'

'Sapna?' Vikram immediately asks.

'Yes, Sapna ... actually Sapna didi. Heard of her?'

The name rings a bell but I can't quite place it.

'She was my best friend,' Ustara says. 'I met her twelve years ago. I was much younger then ... somewhere in 1986.'

Sensing Ustara's absorption with the subject, Vikram stops taking notes and says, 'Tell me more about her.'

Ustara leans back on the couch, lifts his legs to sit cross-legged, and begins speaking.

Chapter 2

THE UNEXPECTED VISITOR

I pulled down the steel handle, opened the closet and sifted through the clothes for my beige cotton trousers. I finally managed to find it after I had thrown all my clothes on the ground. Then, without wasting too much time, I had a bath, shaved and got into my pants before hurriedly shoving all the mess back into the cupboard. When I was ready, I cast one last glance around the room; it was clean enough for the visitor.

That night, I had specifically asked my men to keep away from my house until I called for them. I was going to sleep with a Maharashtrian woman. Not like this was my first time or anything, of course! But this woman, I had been told, was one of a kind. I had already paid a bomb for the whole evening and was anxiously waiting to have her in my bed.

I realised that I had gotten ready an hour before time—

it was only 7.30—so I decided to get myself a drink. I opened a bottle of whiskey and poured a peg in a steel glass. I tried not to make it too strong, pouring more water than usual in it, but before I knew it, I had already thrown it back.

While drinking, I had the wildest thoughts about the girl about to come into my room. My work had deprived me of good nocturnal activity for over two weeks. I wanted to make up for it today. Women have been my weakness ever since I can remember. There is nothing I can really do to get over this, so I just buy them when I have the urge. Today was one such day.

I was already three pegs down and preparing the fourth one, when the doorbell rang. She was here. My heart began thumping and a feeling of anxiety overcame me—for some reason, the excitement to see the woman who I was going to spend the night with had suddenly been overtaken by an ominous feeling. I am generally not a superstitious person, but something did not feel right. I went and opened the door.

To my surprise, instead of a Maharashtrian woman, a lady clad in a shiny black burqa was waiting at the door. Her hands and face were bare, though and—mashallah—I hadn't seen such a beautiful woman at my doorstep in a very long time.

She was tall with milk-like skin. Her lips were a pale pink and she had the most stunning pair of deep-set eyes I had seen. She was worth every single rupee I had spent.

Assuming that she was the Maharashtrian woman in disguise, I called her in.

However, before she entered she said salaam and asked, 'Kya aap Hussain Ustara hain?'

I was startled, first because I did not expect a Hindu to greet me with a salaam, and second, because she knew my name. As far as I remembered, I had strictly informed my men not to mention my name while making the deal. Her beauty though, made me overlook the mistake my men must have made. 'Yes, of course,' I answered. 'Come inside.'

As she walked in, her eyes scanned the room. Then she turned to me and asked, 'Can I sit down? I need to talk to you.'

'Talk?'

From experience, I know that such girls only want to talk first if they want to negotiate a better deal.

'You really want to talk now?' I asked.

'Yes, please hear me out. It is important.'

Her behaviour was strange and that made me suspicious. I told her to sit down and moved towards the drawer where I knew my gun was. I took it out, placed it on the table that was beside her. I have always felt that men with weapons can get the world to touch their feet. I had taken the gun out to intimidate her but she continued to sit there, unflustered. In fact, she merely looked at the gun curiously.

'Can this kill a man?' she asked, her eyes still on the gun.

'Yes, but—'

'How many bullets does this pistol have?' she interrupted me.

'Eighteen. It's made in Germany, and it's my favourite gun. But, why are you so curious about the weapon, sweetheart? I thought you were interested in some other weapon,' I said sarcastically.

'No, I am only interested in weapons that will help me achieve my goal,' she said.

I burst into a fit of laughter, still assuming that she was the Maharashtrian woman I had planned to spend my evening with. 'Goal ... what goal do you have, woman?'

'My goal is the same as yours,' she said.

Aha ... now this pretty lady was talking business, I thought. 'Yes, your goal and mine are possibly the same. The only difference is that you make the money and I lose it on you,' I said.

'Money? I don't make money at all.'

'Oh! So you are doing this for charity, haan?'

'What do you mean?' she looked irritated.

I was tired of this game she was playing, and said so. 'Okay, get on with it woman, stop playing around. Give me what you are here for.'

'I am not here to give you anything. I have nothing to offer, I just want help from you.'

'Help?' I lost my temper and asked angrily, 'What do you want? Who sent you here?'

The woman broke down all of a sudden and began sobbing. I did not know what to do.

'Usmaan bhai sent me here ...' I could hear her say between sobs.

When I heard Usmaan's name, I realised my mistake. Usmaan would never even think of sending a dhandewaali to me. He was too decent a man for that.

I tried to calm her down and rushed to the kitchen to get her a glass of water. When I handed her the glass, she was still weeping.

'Sorry for this. I mistook you for someone else ... Why have you come here?'

'My name is Ashraf Khan. I lost my husband Mehmood Khan last week. He was murdered.'

'I'm really sorry to hear that.'

'I want to settle scores with the man who killed my husband.'

'And who do you think killed your husband?'

'One Dawood from Dubai.'

'Dawood? You mean Dawood Ibrahim?' I asked.

'Yes.'

'And you want to settle scores with him?'

'Yes.'

I wanted to laugh but something in the tone of her voice stopped me. A widow of six days, she did not realise the enormity of her own words. She wanted to take on one of the most dreaded gangsters in the world. 'So, why have you come here?'

'I heard he is your enemy.'

'Yes. If I ever see that rascal, I will feed him alive to the dogs.'

'Then, will you help me kill Dawood?'

'What do you want me to do?'

'Can you teach me how to use a gun?'

I nodded, taken aback by her naivete. Did she honestly believe that was all it took—that because she had lost her husband to guns, that was the only way to get the enemy? Possibly she'll soon realise that she can put her fragile and beautiful self to some better use, I thought. 'Come at noon tomorrow,' I said.

She rose from the couch, thanked me and hurriedly made a move towards the door. I looked at my watch, it was 10 p.m., and there was still no sign of the woman who I had anxiously been waiting to sleep with. Reaching out for the door, Ashraf said, 'Oh, while you were in the kitchen, a woman came to meet you. She saw me and left without saying anything. I tried to stop her ... but she ...'

Oh no! I thought, but only nodded.

'Khuda hafiz, I will come tomorrow,' she said.

There had gone my plans to sleep with a Maharashtrian woman. Ashraf had ruined it all.

Chapter 3

THE AVENGING ANGEL

I jump into the cold water. Inside, my feet touch the tiles before I lunge forward and pull myself upwards. When I reach the surface, I see myself in the middle of a vast pool. The water is a deep, clear blue.

My view however is blocked by three topless Chinese women. They are swirling around me. One is teasing me while the other is trying to pull me towards her. Their bare skin is tanned and their silk-like hair cannot hide their small, supple breasts.

I try reaching for them but they playfully move back, asking me to choose only one. I can't decide. They are all equally tempting. I look from one to the other, at whatever is displayed to me, and then reach for the one whose breasts are fuller. I begin to wade through the water in an attempt to come closer to her. I move my fingers on her lips and come closer to kiss her.

Our lips part but, all of a sudden, her lips move peculiarly and she begins to scowl. She starts screaming frantically. I don't know how to react and I turn around; the other two women have disappeared. I turn back, but this time, instead of the Chinese woman, I see a lady in a shiny burqa. Her face is familiar. She is weeping; her pursed lips slowly open and cry for help. I am scared; I start slipping into the water, only to wake up with a jolt.

When I was awake enough to realise that I'd only had a bad dream, I began to abuse myself for spoiling my own fantasies. Majeed hurriedly walked in just then and told me that a burqewaali was screaming at the door after he had refused to allow her in.

'Send her back. Tell her to come at twelve o'clock. Why the hell has she come so early?'

'Bhai, it is twelve-thirty already,' Majeed said, looking at his watch.

I checked my own watch and saw that he was right. Annoyed, I told him to call her in. 'Get some tea and water,' I said. 'I will be there in five minutes.'

When I entered she was sitting on the same couch that she'd sat on the previous day. Her head was lowered slightly. 'Salaam,' she said.

I returned the greeting but to be honest, I was not happy to see her. I usually avoid beggars, orphans and widows first thing in the day. I personally believe that it is not good luck to start the day seeing their faces.

'Will you have tea?'

'No, I have already eaten at home.'

'I am sorry but I haven't eaten my breakfast yet,' I said, as Majeed walked in with a plate of hot samosas and egg burji. Once again, out of courtesy I asked her if she'd like to have some. Refusing, she got up and walked to the window.

I told Majeed to prepare the targets and get the ghodas to the firing range located in the basement of my building. He agreed but looked at me warily before leaving. Probably, knowing my unhealthy track record with women, he assumed that I was using the poor lady to my advantage.

Ashraf, who was standing near the window, displayed neither anxiety nor excitement. I began eating. I realised that she had turned her face towards the window so that I could eat without feeling embarrassed by her presence. I appreciated this.

As I put the last of the egg burji in my mouth, I asked, 'Are you sure you want to do this?'

'Without a doubt,' she said, now turning her head in my direction.

For the first time, I noticed that her eyes were swollen. It seemed like she hadn't slept a wink and had been crying through the night. I knew that, though I was not interested in helping Ashraf, her despair was pushing me to doing it.

'I need to take revenge, if not for me, for the soul of my husband,' she said.

'Okay, then,' I said with a sigh, as I got up. 'Let's go to the firing range.'

We walked down to the basement. The firing range was

not big enough to contain the jarring sound of gunshots, yet it was not a bad learning ground. Majeed had been efficient enough and placed three targets, two of which were dartboards, and the other a cardboard cut-out. All the three targets were lined at even distance in one corner of the basement. In the middle, Majid had placed a wooden table with three of the best ghodas: a country made-pistol, star pistol and my favourite German Mauser.

'Which one do you want to begin with?' I asked, showing off my pistols to Ashraf.

'The one that will help shoot down my target most effectively.'

I was impressed but didn't respond directly. 'Before I begin, tell me about your fears. Can you bear loud sounds? Are you calm at the sight of blood?'

'Yes.'

'It is very easy to say yes ...'

'When you see your loved one die in front of you, these things don't bother you anymore,' she said curtly.

I turned to Majeed and asked him to bring the glasses and ear-muffs, explaining to her that she needed to wear these since she was an amateur.

She'd never handled a gun before, I could tell. I elaborated on the various parts of the gun, mainly the grip, the trigger guard, the magazine and the barrel. 'Unless and until you are firing, keep your fingers away from the trigger,' I warned.

Then, I lifted my automatic and positioned myself eight

to ten metres away from the first dartboard. I raised my arms straight towards the board and tightened my grip on the gun, placing the index finger of my right hand on the trigger as I did so.

Ashraf watched me very closely. I parted my feet slightly and bent so that the back of my body made a curve. 'When you are still in the learning stage, this is how you position yourself,' I said. 'This position will help you stay balanced when you fire.'

Ashraf nodded and held out her hand impatiently for the gun. I loaded the magazine and handed the gun to her. 'Hold it like I did.'

Her hands dropped slightly with the unexpected weight of the weapon. But, a moment later, she surprised me when she asked me to move aside and confidently took the same position as mine. She was still in her burqa, and that made me very uncomfortable. But as she bent slightly, I realised that she was imitating the stance I'd shown her perfectly.

'Wait, this is not enough. You need to cock the weapon first.'

She looked confused. I smiled at her innocence, took the gun from her and moved several metres away.

'Watch me.' I grasped the slide on top of the pistol and pulled it towards me. When, I had drawn it back fully, I released it. There was a 'click' sound.

'The gun is ready to fire now,' I said.

Taking my previous position once again, I fired two rounds. One of the bullets hit the centre of the target. I realised I was relieved; I didn't want Ashraf to think I was not capable.

I handed the gun to her and warned her of the sound and the jolt she'd receive.

'I am not afraid,' she retorted.

She held the gun and placed her index finger on the trigger.

'Now, remember, don't pull, just squeeze it slowly,' I said.

Her finger squeezed the trigger slowly. A gunshot fired in the air and Ashraf fell back from the force with which the gun recoiled.

'You can't afford to be that delicate.' I reached out to help her regain her balance.

'I'll manage on my own; I don't like men touching me,' she said.

Offended, I said harshly, 'If that is so, then you shouldn't be with a stranger during your iddat period in the first place.' Iddat is the three-month period of mourning that Muslims widows follow. During this time, the women usually don't meet or talk to men outside their family.

Ashraf ignored me. 'I want to try this once more,' she said.

I shrugged and walked to the stool in the corner, annoyed by her coldness.

On that same day, Ashraf managed to progress quite a bit, in the art of shooting. We completed our first day's training session at 4 p.m. I was hungry but she was showing no signs of leaving. 'This is enough for one day. Don't stress yourself too much. But you need to practise with the same intensity every day.'

I invited her to join me for lunch but she refused.

'No thank you Hussain bhai. What time tomorrow?'

'First, please stop calling me "bhai", I don't like it. About the next session, we shall meet at the same time tomorrow. Khuda hafiz,' I said and stomped out of the firing range.

Over the next few days, she perfected the use of the gun. We were in the basement and Ashraf had completed her two-hour shooting session. I was sitting on the stool and watching her pack up. When she finished, she walked towards me with a brown haversack hanging from her right shoulder and asked innocently, 'I guess this would be enough to take on Dawood? When do we go to Dubai?'

I managed to control my laughter. 'Are you prepared to take on someone physically?'

'No.'

'Then I guess your training is not over yet,' I said teasingly.

'So, let's learn. What are we waiting for?' she asked, irritated.

I was astonished: she was behaving as if I were obligated to teach her or as if she were my sole priority in life at the moment. 'Listen,' I said, 'I have a lot of work. You should be thankful that I'm making time for you at all.'

She seemed chagrined. 'I'm sorry,' she said.

Immediately, I melted. 'Anyway … I can give you some basic ideas on self-defence today. We can work on the rest tomorrow when I'll introduce you to my martial arts trainer.'

Ashraf dropped the haversack and stood to hear me out carefully.

'Just a few rules …' I said. 'Always remember that there are three parts in your body which you can use for your defence: your elbows, knees and heels. Even if you are injured, these three will always remain functional.'

'How can I best use them when fighting against a man?'

I looked at her for a long time, not knowing how to frame my sentence. Finally, I said, 'Between a man's legs.'

There was a long and awkward silence between the two of us. I was trying to phrase the sentences in my mind so that she wouldn't feel uncomfortable.

'Not there as you are thinking … I meant the … uh … testicles. I mean, somewhere below the crotch. Men usually are rendered helpless for a good ten minutes; by this time, you can escape.'

She stared at me for a few seconds. Then she lifted her haversack and looked at me again. I thought that I had offended her and was about to apologise, when she broke into a half-smile. 'We shall meet tomorrow. Thank you.'

I was relieved; I returned her smile with one of my own.

Two weeks passed and Ashraf was picking up well. We met every day: she even insisted on being taught on Sundays. I found it hard to say no to her. While she remained the same burqa-clad, aloof woman I had first met, I began to have feelings for her. And it only intensified on the day when we had our first big fight.

I had decided to teach Ashraf to ride a motorbike. I was riding with her when her burqa got stuck in the rod of a truck. It was a near-death experience and I told her that it would be impossible for her to learn to ride a bike if she had a burqa on. In fact, I tried to explain how simple things would be if she behaved more sensibly and did not wear the burqa in the first place.

She was infuriated and we had a big argument. After a lot of quarrelling, Ashraf stormed out angrily. The next day, when Majeed woke me up, I was surprised and shocked to see her in my drawing room, dressed in a salwaar kameez. She was beautiful, more beautiful than I'd thought.

Uff ... what a distraction she could be. I felt like I was falling in love with her.

'Hussain sahib, let's learn to ride the bike,' she said.

'You finally agreed.'

'Of course I had to,' she said, giving me her beautiful smile. 'I will do anything for Mehmood.'

Chapter 4

ASHRAF'S REINCARNATION

After two months of our rigorous training sessions, Ashraf had learned the art of self-defence, the use of weaponry and had been confidently riding around the city on my bike.

Ashraf had changed. From salwar-kameezes, she had moved to wearing jeans and long, loose shirts. Her monosyllabic replies had also been replaced with sharp and witty remarks. I soon realised that she was a wordsmith: articulate and linguistically gifted. Also, unlike before, Ashraf was filled less with sorrow and more with the desire to get her revenge.

We had gotten quite close and it was impossible for her not to have realised my affection for her, yet she never said anything.

One afternoon, Ashraf excused herself from a training session for some 'legal work'.

Feeling a little lost without her, I thought of taking a

ride down to Marine Drive. However, just minutes before I could leave home, Ashraf walked in. I was more than delighted to see her.

'Mubarak ho, Hussain sahib,' she said, removing her chappals and walking into my bedroom. She was holding some papers.

'What happened? You seem very happy,' I asked, trying to hide my pleasure on seeing her.

'Yes, I am. There is so much to tell you.'

'Do you want to take a ride to Marine Drive,' I asked, adding, 'we can talk about it there.' She agreed.

This time, she rode while I sat pillion, and I must confess that the ride was as smooth as satin. She stopped the bike at a parking lot in Nariman Point and locked it. Then she got off and shoved some papers from her handbag into my hands. I was still sitting on the bike.

'What's this?'

'Read it.'

'You know I don't have the patience, Ashraf.'

'Okay ... but promise me you won't get angry,' she said.

'What is it about?'

'Remember this morning I called to tell you that I won't be in because of some legal matter?'

I nodded.

'Actually my lawyer had called ...' she said a little timidly as if she had been hiding a thing or two for a long time.

'Lawyer ... what for?'

'My petition against police inspector Emanuel Amolik is going to come up for hearing in the high court soon.'

'What? When did you file the petition?' I asked, surprised.

'I'm sorry, I know I didn't inform you about this before, but after seeking advice from a relative, I had filed a petition against Amolik in the high court last month,' she said, sounding guilty. 'Luckily, the case is coming up for hearing soon.'

I was baffled. It was not going to be easy for a young woman to take on a senior Crime Branch officer like Amolik. Also, for a court already clogged with so many pending cases, I wondered how her petition could actually see the light of day so soon.

'So, what is the good news in this?' I asked.

'Well, this is going to make things easy for both of us from here on, won't it?'

'How?' I asked, mystified.

'See, if the court passes an order against Amolik, Dawood will be netted for his involvement, too. Then, we won't have to go all the way to Dubai to kill him as he will be brought to the city following the court's orders.'

Oh, God ... she was so naive. I shook my head, hating to have to disappoint her. 'If that were the case, then Dawood would have been here long ago. There are so many warrants and summons pending against him; yet he is still in Dubai, a free man. You think a petition against an encounter specialist will bring him back?'

Ashraf's face fell. 'Oh! But I was told ...' She wanted to say something but couldn't continue.

Suddenly, an idea occurred to me. I came closer to her and whispered, 'Dawood has a chain of gambling dens, protection and extortion rackets. His money is channelled by hawala from dance bars, nightclubs, film productions, etc. Find a way to stop the flow of money from these ... he is sure to feel the pinch.'

She paused for a second, trying to absorb what I'd told her. 'Can you tell me how to go about this?' she asked.

For the first time, I would be revealing the actual nature of my job—the dark undercurrents of what I did for a living.

Perhaps trusting her too much, I said, 'Ashraf, I have for a long time been working as an informer only to get at Dawood. My networks feed me with information about his new businesses. I pass this on to the cops. The cops, if they succeed in doing something about it, give me a small percentage of the profits.'

Seemingly unaffected by what I had just told her, Ashraf said, 'I am willing to do the same, if that will make life difficult for him. But first, how do I begin?'

I looked around; it was late afternoon and Marine Drive was fairly empty except for a few college students. I inched closer to her. 'Align with his enemies. Befriend all his detractors, just like you got hold of me. They will help you. As of now, Arun Gawli seems to be the best way to crack down on Dawood's business. Heard of him?' I asked.

'No,' she said curtly. She was uncomfortable with my proximity, I realised, so I stepped back.

'Gawli is a big ganglord, a Hindu. He lives in Dagdi Chawl in Byculla, and Dawood and he are constantly waging war against each other.'

'Do you know him?' she asked.

'No. I don't know him personally.'

She walked towards the promenade and stood facing the sea for five minutes. I realised that she did not want to be disturbed. When she came back, I was sitting on the bike munching channa that I had bought from a hawker.

'I am going now. I shall take a bus. Thank you once again. Khuda haafiz,' she said and walked towards Mantralaya to take a bus from the depot. I sat for some time, by myself, thinking about how Ashraf was slowly taking over my life. After a restless half-hour, I started my bike and left for home.

The next day, Ashraf was her usual self at the training session, totally focused on the martial arts exercises we were doing. I, on the other hand, was completely distracted by her presence. I wanted to hold her, and feel her body against mine but I knew that she would not allow me to have any of her now. If ever.

Suddenly, she stopped and said, 'I met Gawli.'

'What did he say?' I asked, trying not to sound flustered by how quickly she'd acted on my suggestion.

'He listened to me patiently. However, I think he is suspicious about my being Dawood's agent or something.

Also, he doesn't seem to think that aligning with a woman is the safest thing.'

'So?'

'He turned down my offer. He said that although he is supportive of all those who are against Dawood, in my case he cannot do much except feel sorry for me and my husband.'

'Well, at least you tried. I'm proud of you.'

She picked up a water bottle that was lying on a table, took a sip, and after a pregnant pause said, 'But I have thought of something. It may sound foolish but I think that it is the only way forward.'

'What is it?' I asked.

'I have decided to change my name,' she said calmly.

'And why is that?'

'After yesterday's encounter with Gawli, I have realised that these Hindu gangsters don't trust Muslim women easily. I need to have a name that sounds more Hindu,' she said.

I pointed out that Gawli himself had married a Muslim woman.

'But even she has a Hindu name now,' she retorted. 'I met her. Her name is Asha and she is a Hindu now.'

'So have you thought of a name?' I asked.

'No, not yet,' she said, and then, after a pause, 'It is my dream to kill Dawood. It is the only thing I think about night and day.'

'How is that related to this?' I asked.

'It's my sapna … I think I'll call myself Sapna … dream … and Sapna, after all, is a name acceptable to both Hindus and Muslims,' she said.

'Not bad,' I said, adding, 'so from today Ashraf is Sapna. To celebrate, we should both eat biryani.' She laughed. I was happy for her.

From then on, Ashraf began to be called Sapna. She used this name when dealing with Hindu gangsters and the Mumbai police.

Even before I realised it, Sapna had made major inroads into the underworld. She would move around the dark streets of Mumbai well past midnight and build on contacts that I initially helped her out with. She collected details about the dance bars and gambling dens in the city, and the moment she realised that they were in some way or the other connected to the underworld or Dawood, she would tip off Crime Branch officers.

All this while, Sapna refused to reveal her identity to the cops. She preferred anonymity and would only divulge information on the phone, calling them from telephone booths across the city. She even refused to collect her rewards following the crackdown by the police.

In a few weeks, Sapna managed to close down several dens in the city. During this time, Sapna was still a regular at the training sessions but apart from asking me for information on Dawood's activities in the city, she rarely discussed how she was going about getting things done. However, my men, who had been keeping watch on her, told me what she was doing. One day, Rafeeq, one of my most trusted aides, told me how, following Sapna's tip-off, the police had rounded up over forty persons. Tadipaar* orders were served to around twenty of them, and several others were still in trouble. He also told me that two of Dawood's gambling dens had been sealed by the police.

In three weeks, Sapna had managed to do what I would have never been able to do. Before she put herself in a more dangerous position, I decided to talk to her as she had unknowingly been gaining enemies.

We decided to meet for dinner. I had already reserved a table for two at my favourite Iranian restaurant. When I reached the AC room, it was empty except for a family with annoying kids hovering around. As expected, Sapna, who for a change was dressed in a burqa, was already there.

After we'd said our salaams and ordered our food, I decided to broach the subject. 'Ashraf, there is something I need to talk to you about.'

'Sapna,' she corrected.

'Okay, Sapna. I've heard of your work as an informer. I also heard that you've been doing a good job.'

'Yes, if it all works as I planned, we will be able to get the person we want soon,' she said.

'No, Sapna, unfortunately that is not true,' I said.

'Why?' she asked, startled.

'You don't know the risks involved in your job. You

* Removed from the city, 'tadipaar' in police lingo.

are still fresh in the business; it is beside the point that you have started off very well,' I explained.

'I know the risks. I have already been attacked twice.'

'What? And you chose not to tell me this?' The spoonful of rice I had just eaten almost choked me.

'It is okay ... with your training I managed to stop them. I kicked the rascals in their manhood. They were at a loss for words.'

'And you escaped?' I asked, relieved but annoyed.

'How do you think I am having dinner with you?' she mocked, and continued to eat her food.

I had to bring her down to earth. She did not know what she was doing, and by the time she realised it, it could be too late. I was too fond of Sapna to lose her to her own stupid actions. And perhaps, I was upset that she didn't seem to need me much anymore.

'Are you mad? When will you grow up, Sapna? Do you think Dawood is going to feel the pinch if you bust his gambling and dance bars business? He is too big. All he has to do is shoot you in the head and your story will be over,' I said angrily. 'Most of his money comes from protection and extortion rackets. Have you managed to trace these rackets?'

'No.'

'Then why are you rejoicing?' I asked.

'I'll be able to trace them if you stop yelling at me and guide me instead.'

'You think if I knew this, I'd spare him? It is done

through hawala and not easy to trace. But I recently got a tip-off on Dawood's arms consignment and fake currency racket. And from what I know, this involves big money.'

'What about it?' she asked excitedly.

'Normally, most of the arms and fake currency comes to Indian from Pakistan but via the Kathmandu border. I know of some people like Ram Singh Bahadur who is well- connected and knows where and when Dawood's consignment will come in. Are you interested?'

'Do you mean we go to Nepal?'

'Yes. I have a plan. All I want to know is whether you are game for such a huge assignment. Even if we manage to plunder one or two of his consignments in Nepal, we can cause immense losses to Dawood,' I said. 'And then he will know we are in the fray.'

Chapter 5

THE MACABRE EXCURSION

That Sapna was willing to travel across the border with a man other than her husband spoke of her determination to achieve her goal.

I called a friend of mine, Ram Bahadur Singh, and he told me that he had learned about a weaponry consignment being channelled to Kathmandu later that week. This meant that we would have to make our plans and act on them quickly.

Sapna and I decided to take a route that would enable us to intercept the consignment after it passed Kathmandu, somewhere in the hilly regions of Birganj, where the Border Security Forces would be less concentrated. In order to familiarise ourselves with the place, I decided that we would first go to Kathmandu via Birganj, gather some intelligence and then return to Birganj, where we could intercept Dawood's consignment.

But the journey to Birganj was going to be arduous; we would first have to travel to Raxaul, a small town in Bihar, and then take the bus to Birganj. Raxaul is also the hub for cross-border smuggling—be it arms, electronic goods, drugs or fake currency, you could find everything there.

I cannot forget those few days that I spent with Sapna. The journey was tiring but every second spent with her was worth its weight in gold. Before this, I had never really cared for any woman. With Sapna it was different, because though I always wanted to make love to her, I realised that I wanted more; it went beyond lust.

During the journey, Sapna spoke to me about a lot of things, like her life after Mehmood, her plans to remarry, have children, etc. It was the first time she opened her heart out to me. She was no longer a grieving widow and I began to see that there was more to her, apart from her determination to avenge the death of her husband.

Also, unlike before, she was interested in finding out about me as a person, rather than someone who was just there to help her accomplish her goal.

'Why do people call you Hussain Ustara? I mean, when Usmaan bhai first told me about you, I thought that you had a scar on your face or something,' she said.

I liked it that she was curious about me.

'The truth is that I was never scarred. Others gave me the name after an incident that dates back to some two decades ago,' I explained.

'What happened then?'

'I was about fifteen then, and into picking pockets. A gang of us would jump into crowded buses, trains, theatres and do our work—and mind you, I was among the best of the lot. The cops would rarely catch me. Once, I got hold of a lot of cash. Tempted, I only gave part of my day's collection to my ringleader, who took stock of the money we made on a daily basis. But when he learned how I had duped him through one of my friends, he beat me up. I tried retaliating with the help of a few others and it blew up into a full-fledged skirmish inside the club where we had assembled.'

'Then?' she prompted.

'Then ... then when I realised that things were going out of control, and I had no means to escape. I removed my razor from inside my pocket and attacked the ringleader. I managed to inflict a wound that began at his neck and ran right to his crotch.'

'Yah Allah. Are you serious?'

I nodded. 'He was bleeding a lot and I managed to get away. He was taken to a hospital and the doctor there made a strange remark. He said that the person who had cut him had done so with surgical precision. And soon, before I could realise it, the name Ustara got stuck to my name. From then on people started fearing me, all because of that small weapon ...'

When we reached Kathmandu, I introduced Sapna to Raamu and Chaamu Singh, my friends from Nepal who often supplied me with weapons. I wanted to check the accuracy of the intelligence about Dawood's consignment that had been given to me by Ram Bahadur Singh. Bahadur was right. Chaamu Singh told me that Kim Bahadur Thapa, Dawood's trusted lieutenant who operates from Mumbai's Matunga area, was supposed to send some consignment to Raxaul via Birganj. And that one of their men would be at the border to collect the consignment, which would reach Birganj in the next three days. This was the right time to hit out at Dawood. I sat down with the three of them and drew a rough chart, planning where we would intercept the arms consignment. We decided that we'd get down a few kilometres before Birganj and walk the rest of the distance, taking the kachcha road through the mountainous terrain. I personally felt that it would be easier to hide near the hillocks and seize the consignment that would be transported to the borders using mules or donkeys. The others agreed. 'Will this affect Dawood's business?' Sapna asked.

'No, not so soon,' I replied, and explained to Sapna that while the seizure was big, it would take a few more such attacks before Dawood would feel the hole in his pocket and be alarmed.

After two days, which we spent working out the details of the heist, we headed for Birganj. Raamu Singh drove us in a car to the spot we had decided on. From there on, it was only Sapna and me. We walked on the rough terrain of Birganj for some time and finally managed to find the route taken by smugglers. We chose to hide behind a massive nine-foot rock. All that we had with us were some dry fruits, water-bottles, a torch, a long rope and our automatic pistols. I knew that the wait was going to be long.

At around 5.30 in the evening, I heard the sound of hooves. I peeped around the rock to see three Nepali men with donkeys that were carrying heavy loads on their backs. One of the gunny sacks was pointed at both ends. There was no doubt that AK-47s had been rolled inside it. This had to be them.

I shook Sapna by her shoulders; she had drifted off to sleep. When she opened her eyes, I pulled out the German Mausers from my bag, loaded the magazines and handed one to her. Again, I looked around the rock and this time spotted a heavily-built, dark man behind the Nepalis.

I gestured to Sapna to stand behind me. The noise of the hooves began getting louder; now we could also hear the men whisper in their local language. I held Sapna by her hand and slipped out from our spot to face them. I withdrew my hand from hers and pointed my gun at them. She did the same. The men, as expected, were taken aback. They looked at each other before one of them fearlessly came forward.

'Whoever you are, back off or you will simply get yourselves killed,' the man said in broken Hindi.

I took a few steps forward and released my right hand from the grip of the gun to slap him hard across his face. 'The gun is in my hand, so don't threaten me with death,' I said, holding him by the collar. The other men remained still.

Suddenly, my head exploded with pain: someone had come up from behind and hit me with something. I fell to the ground, face-first, one of my hands reaching for my head. I'd managed to retain my grip on my gun, though.

When I turned around, a huge man came up and stood astride me, his legs holding my body still. He was the same man I'd seen walking behind the others—I hadn't realised that he wasn't around when I had accosted them. He swung at me with the lathi he was holding and then lifted his right foot to kick me hard on the stomach. At that moment, I knew I was staring death in the face.

The other men came up and started hitting me with their lathis as well. I tried to defend myself against the heavy charge of sticks but to no avail. Though it was impossible to escape, I did not want to die so cheaply. In all this, I had completely forgotten about Sapna. The last time I'd seen her was when I pulled her out to face the men; after that everything had happened so quickly. Sapna's absence had not occurred to me until just then. If these bastards caught her, God knows what they would do to her.

Still lying on the ground, I first moved left and then right, trying to locate her amidst the kicks and lashes. I couldn't see her anywhere. Had they tied her up or had she managed to escape? Slowly, I began to feel like I was sinking; I'd stopped trying to hold off the attacking lathis, a while back. Suddenly, one of the men hit me hard on my knees and my upper body lunged forward. My eyes fell straight across, far beyond all of them, towards the donkeys that had been with them. Sapna was standing there, positioned awkwardly. I had a faint idea of what she was going to do. She must have managed to slink away while they had nabbed me.

Sapna later told me that she had lifted her right leg and kicked the first donkey hard on his genitals, and had done the same with the other two within the gap of a few seconds. The startled donkeys—in much pain—instantly ran towards us, braying. Confused by the noise and sudden movement, all the four men moved in different directions.

Taking advantage of the situation, Sapna fired a bullet in the air. I, too, ignoring the pain in my body, lifted myself to pick up my gun. Struggling to get a grip, I fired my gun towards the man who had earlier caught me off-guard. To my luck, the bullet pierced through his forearm. We had the advantage now.

We asked them to drop their lathis and tied them tight to each other with some rope. I wanted to kill them but Sapna pulled me away. Leaving the men to fend for themselves, we left the place with the donkeys.

When we reached an isolated region, somewhere in the dense mountains of Birganj, almost 3,000 metres above sea-level, we slit open the gunny sacks to discover four pistols and three AK47s. 'We can go to Kolkata and sell this to the underworld there. We'll make huge profits,' I said.

'I have no intention of making money with this crap.'

'Are you crazy? You don't realise the money we can make,' I said, my voice still hoarse with pain.

She looked at me, and said angrily, 'I want this stuff destroyed and I want to do it now.'

'That's impossible. We'll need to go to the city and destroy the guns with the help of an ironsmith or something.'

'No one is going anywhere.' Saying this, she put all the weaponry in one sack and threw it over the side of the cliff.

'How much harm have we caused Dawood?'

'Like I told you before, nothing significant,' I said, irritated. I was upset and angry that she hadn't listened to me. We could have made lakhs of rupees if we had sold this consignment. She hadn't even noticed that my clothes were soaked with blood from the wounds those men had inflicted on me. As if she had read my mind, the expression on her face changed. She came up to me, and for the first time, touched my face with her soft hands. 'Sorry for putting you through all this. I don't know how to thank you.'

My anger melted instantaneously. 'It is okay, Sapna. I am doing this because I care for you.'

'I care for you, too,' she said. Tears of happiness rolled down her face. Her first major plan to inflict harm to Dawood had been successful.

Chapter 6

THE A-TEAM SPLITS

Forty-eight months had gone by since our first trip to Nepal and there had been a lot of changes in both our lives in that time.

After our first success, Sapna and I—at least for the first few months—visited Nepal often. On some occasions we failed miserably, and at others, we managed to get hold of huge consignments. Eventually—after I convinced her that the money could help in her mission against Dawood—Sapna no longer rebuffed my suggestion of selling the stolen weaponry in the markets of Kolkata and Raxaul. We were thus successful on two levels: in hampering Dawood's business, and monetarily too.

Then, one day, we came in direct contact with the Border Security Forces in Nepal. That encounter nearly resulted in our deaths. Fortunately, we somehow managed to escape, and Sapna decided to call off our Nepal trips for good. I was reluctant, since we were getting a lot of money this way but she refused to budge. So, after a lot of arguing, I finally gave in and agreed to keep Mumbai our sole base against Dawood.

In Mumbai, Sapna was slowly gaining notice as the person responsible for disrupting Dawood's businesses. She knew the Mumbai underworld like the back of her hand and was creating unprecedented fear in the minds of Dawood's many henchmen. She had begun to play a big role in busting several gambling dens and dance bars in the city as well.

The only major setback Sapna suffered was something I had predicted—her only legal route to justice had been quashed by the court. The Crime Branch, on the basis of Sapna's allegations, did conduct a farcical inquiry against Inspector Amolik. However, the inspector was finally given a clean chit and her case was dismissed for lack of evidence. But Sapna never gave up. She continued to file petition after petition. She was confident that her dream, just as her name suggested, would see the light of day. I loved her too much to discourage her.

While time had brought about so many changes in our position and in Sapna's position in the underworld, things remained the same with regard to my feelings for her and vice versa. No doubt we had become very close friends, sometimes I felt we could even read each other's minds. We quarrelled, we laughed and dined together almost every day. She knew all about the women I slept with and would keep asking me to change my ways. I knew she enjoyed spending time with me—but that's all it was; there was never the hint of her wanting anything more. She couldn't think beyond Mehmood.

I knew that she was aware of my feelings but she continued to feign ignorance. It annoyed me sometimes, and—like anyone would—I too, was reaching a point where I didn't think I could take it any longer. I was just hoping that it wouldn't happen soon.

But it did. Something terrible happened one day, after which she was forced to part ways with me. I admit it was all my fault.

It was December 1991, at around 2 a.m. I was at home, bored ... I hadn't felt like paying a woman for sex that night. It was just one of those off days when I did not want to have any fun. Such days, however, had only occurred after Sapna came into my life. I guess I wanted to prove to her that I could be faithful.

I was lying on my couch, listening to some old Hindi songs from the '60s on my radio but my mind was on Sapna. I imagined making love to her, placing my lips on her navel and then slowly moving upwards to press her lips against mine and kissing her passionately. I was in some kind of trance and didn't realise when I had fallen asleep.

I must have been in a deep sleep when someone started shaking me hurriedly. I opened my eyes and saw Sapna standing before me. She was panting and weeping.

Sapna had an extra key to my home, as she usually

Jenabai's ancestral home in Chunawala Building in Dongri, in its current state. Jenabai first shifted to the first floor of the building at fourteen, when she married Mohammad Shah Darwesh, a small-time businessman, in the early 1940s. Though she made enough money as an informer and bootlegger, she refused to leave the building and breathed her last here in 1993.

Haji Mastan's bungalow, Baitul Suroor, on Peddar Road, where Jenabai brought Mumbai's warring gangsters together in 1980, in order to have them come to a truce.

پاکستان بنتے ہی شوہر چھوڑ کر پاکستان بھاگ گیا اور جینابائی زندگی سے لڑنے کیلئے اکیلی رہ گئی

اخبار عالم

بمبئی کے داداؤں نے جینابائی کے آگے ہتھیار کیوں ڈالے؟

A front page interview of Jenabai Daaruwali in one of the most prominent Urdu newspapers, *Akbhar-e-Alam*, in 1992, a year before her death.

Kamathipura 12th Lane, where Gangubai lived during the last few years of her life. Journalists and ministers would come to meet Gangubai here.

A framed picture of Gangubai, which is seen in most homes and brothels in the red-light area. She is revered like a goddess.

After Gangubai's death, busts were made in her memory and installed in Kamathipura, in brothels that were under her jurisdiction.

Drug baroness Jyoti Adiramlingam controls the drug trafficking network in Reay Road in Central Mumbai with an iron fist. Jyoti used to be part of the infamous troika (Savitri, Jyoti and Papamani) of women, who dominated the narcotics industry in Mumbai in the early 1990s. This photograph was procured from Jyoti's family album by the Narcotics Control Bureau (NCB).

An old photograph of Mahalaxmi Papamani, sourced from the NCB. Despite several attempts, we were unable to procure a recent picture of her.

Gangster Abu Salem and Bollywood starlet Monica Bedi (right) seen sharing a lighter moment with friends and family. The couple was eventually arrested in Lisbon on 20 September 2002 for entering Portugal with forged documents.

These are the photos acquired from the passports of Danish Beg, alias Abu Salem, and Fauzia Beg, alias Monica Bedi. The couple used these names for fake passports, which they later used to travel abroad.

Asha Gawli, the wife of Hindu don Arun Gawli, who shielded her husband against police machinery and fake encounters on several occasions, is seen appealing to the masses to vote for her husband from the Byculla constituency, before the Maharashtra Legislative Assembly elections in October 2009. (Courtesy: *Indian Express*, Mumbai)

Late Shiv Sena corporator Neeta Naik, who convinced and encouraged her electronics graduate husband Ashwin Naik to join the underworld, posing for lensmen inside her flat at Subashnagar, Byculla. In 2000, Ashwin got his henchmen to gun his wife down outside her home. (Courtesy: *Mid-Day*, Mumbai)

Sujata Nikhalje, the ambitious wife of self-proclaimed patriotic don Chhota Rajan, walks out of a Maharashtra Control of Organised Crime Act (MCOCA) court after a hearing. (Courtesy: *Mid-Day*, Mumbai)

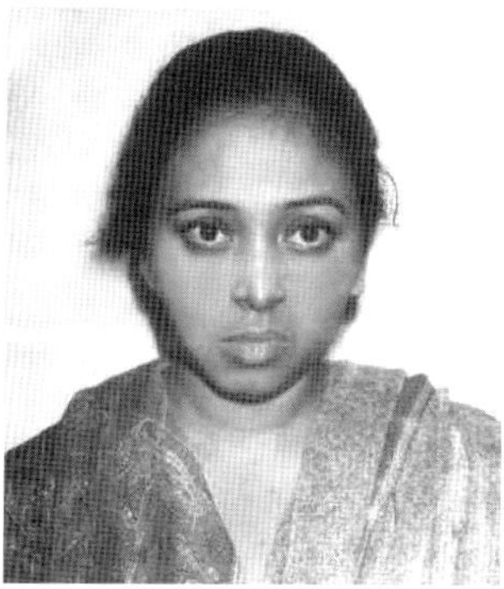

Padma Poojary, the alleged mastermind behind notorious gangster Ravi Poojary, has been absconding ever since she was let out on bail in a passport forgery case in 2005. A five-year-old Interpol Red Corner notice is still pending against her. (Courtesy: CBI website)

Shameem Mirza Beg, alias Mrs Paul, was Chhota Shakeel's business cum love interest. Apart from spending hours talking to the Karachi-based don on the phone, she also managed and supervised his activities in Mumbai. She was arrested in March 2002 under the stringent MCOCA and chargesheeted three months later. (Courtesy: *Mid-Day*, Mumbai)

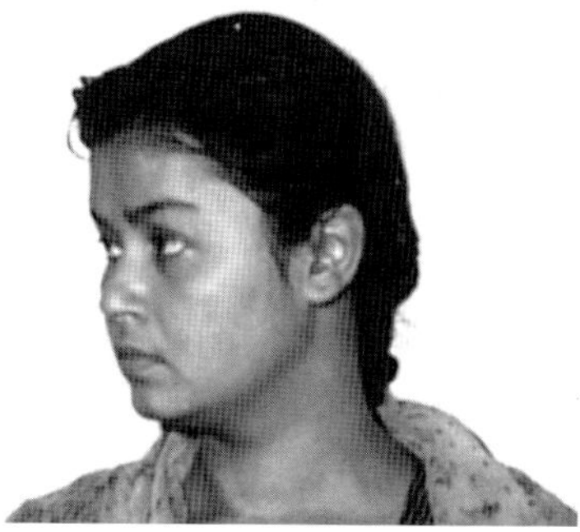

Rubina Siraj Sayyed, notoriously referred to as the moti (fat) girlfriend of Chhota Shakeel, is seen coming out of the Mumbai Crime Branch office. Once a beautician, Rubina allegedly looked after all the needs of Shakeel's gangsters and handled the financial affairs of his gang. She was convicted under MCOCA. (Courtesy: *Mid-Day*, Mumbai)

Mumbai's most famous bar girl, Tarannum Khan, of Deepa Bar, made headlines when the police found out that she had minted millions from betting on international cricket games. (Courtesy: *Mid-Day*, Mumbai)

came over early in the morning to prepare breakfast for me. I looked at my watch—it was 2.30 in the morning. My half- drunk glass of whiskey was still lying on the table. Sapna was in a green salwaar-kameez, and her long, silky hair was dishevelled. Her dupatta was also missing.

'So late? What happened?' I asked, a little dazed.

'A gang of goondas are after me, please help me.'

'But what happened?' I asked again, looking for a shirt to cover my bare chest.

'I was outside a gambling den, on one of my usual recces. One of them recognised me ...' she said. 'I tried to run but they were ten, twelve of them. I managed to come here and I think they saw me enter the building.'

'No one can harm you if I am around. Sit down.' I put on my shirt, took my German Mauser and asked her to sit quietly. Then, locking my house, I went down to scan the area. I couldn't find anyone. Perhaps they hadn't tracked her to my building; in any case, even if they had, I knew they would not have dared to do anything. When I returned inside, Sapna, who was sitting on the chair, still looked terrified.

'Don't worry, I drove them away,' I lied.

'Hussain sahib ... I thought they were going to rape me ...' she said, her hands shaking. I had never seen her so scared.

I don't know what happened to me but at that moment, I just took her by the hand, pulled her up from the chair and hugged her. She did not resist, and I thought that she had finally given in to my and her own desire. So I reached around to unzip her kurta with one hand, while, with the other, I made to cup her breast. Sapna realised what was happening and pushed me away so hard, I fell to the ground.

'What the hell are you trying to do?' she screamed. 'I thought you were my friend! Instead you tried to take advantage of my situation today!' I don't think Sapna could believe what I had done.

'Listen,' I said, lifting myself from the floor, 'don't get me wrong. I just lost control ...'

'Control? I always knew you treated women like whores but I thought that you treated me with a bit more respect. I was wrong ...' Sapna was livid.

'Stop talking rubbish. If I wanted, I could have had you long back ... but I didn't.'

'You have a mind filled with filth. I should have expected this behaviour from you long ago.'

Hurt by her stinging words, I said, 'All these years, it was I who helped you become a somebody. And I have been meaning to tell you what you are actually ... you are just a shrewd, scheming bitch who—'

Before I could even complete my sentence, Sapna came towards me and slapped me hard across the face. Her eyes had turned red. 'I don't think we can ever be together after what happened today. But I will never forget what you have done for me. Khuda hafiz.'

She walked towards the door, turned the knob and

stormed out of my house, slamming the door behind her. I ran behind her, down the building, telling her it was not safe to be out alone at that hour but she ignored me. I watched as she crossed the road, got into a taxi and drove away.

That was the last time I saw Sapna.

At first, I did not try and get in touch with her, thinking that she would eventually cool down and forgive my behaviour. But over six months passed and there was absolutely no news from her. All this while, my men kept me updated about her activities and whereabouts, so I knew she was safe. I would be lying, though, if I said that I didn't miss her every single day of my life. Unfortunately, there was nothing that could be done. If she didn't want to approach me, there was no way I could go to her.

Our separation did nothing to affect her plans against Dawood, though. In fact, after we parted ways, I was told that she assembled a group of Muslim youth in her struggle against the mafia, and Dawood in particular. Her group of young men treated her with a lot of respect. For them, she was like their older sister, which is why they addressed her as didi. Sapna had drilled into them her cause of defeating Dawood, who she believed was a stigma to the Muslim community. Her men served as a strong network of informers, and in the name of Mehmood, she continued to do what she believed in strongly.

Then, one day, about two years after we parted, one of my men, Ahmed, who on my insistence had been keeping track of Sapna's activities, shocked me when he told me that Sapna was in the middle of plotting a very audacious plan, which if executed, could lead to Dawood's funeral. Ahmed had got the tip-off from one of Sapna's trusted aides.

Sapna, like always, had managed to surprise me. The plan, which I still consider exemplary, took me off-balance. Like everyone else in India, Sapna wasn't spared the brouhaha surrounding the India–Pakistan cricket matches being played in Sharjah in the early 1990s. Sapna wasn't a cricket fan; if she watched these matches, she did it only for one person—the rotund man who sat in the VIP enclosure with his glares on, unruffled by media scrutiny. Sapna hadn't seen Dawood in person before, and these matches were the only time when he actually came out in public. Sapna watched each and every move he made. Ahmed had told me that she had recorded most of these matches and was in the process of getting a blueprint of the Sharjah Cricket Association Stadium. Yes, Sapna was planning to kill Dawood at the stadium, in front of thousands of people, while a match was going on.

I remember Sapna telling me once that the Nepal trips and constant tip-offs to the police were not really helping her accomplish anything. She felt her efforts were a drop in the ocean of Dawood's underworld business. Perhaps this was true but we'd heard that Dawood was very annoyed that someone was daring to challenge his supremacy. That it was Mehmood's wife and I, had made him doubly annoyed. But this hadn't satisfied Sapna and perhaps it had only been a matter of time before she decided to take this step.

As far as I know, Sapna had never been to Dubai or Sharjah. If she knew anything about these places, it could have been only through her husband. Sapna had hand- picked around seven to ten men. Ahmed told me that Sapna had made arrangements to send these men for a brief trip to get an idea of the place before they carried out the attack. She was confident that Dawood would be unarmed at the stadium. According to the game plan, the men would carry innocuous tools like umbrellas, glass bottles and stilettos to the stadium and buy tickets for seats around the VIP enclosure where Dawood would be sitting. At a point when the audience stood up to cheer a six, or a wicket taken, some of Sapna's men would handle Dawood's men, while the rest—using the sharp tips of the umbrellas and broken bottles—would attack and kill Dawood. The whole thing, Sapna hoped, would only last a few minutes.

Chapter 7

REVENGE GONE AWRY

Sometimes I wonder if I could ever forgive myself for what I did to her. Our parting had been so acrimonious that she had not once thought of meeting me again. I wanted to stand by her as she prepared to take on Dawood but she had left no room for me in her life. I heard that Sapna had married a cop from Nagpada. Apparently they'd developed a great rapport during her years as a police informer. It hurt me to learn that she was with someone else but knowing Sapna, I guessed that she had some agenda behind this too. As I predicted, her marriage did not last long.

Meanwhile, her men—after travelling to Sharjah—had made all the necessary arrangements, including sourcing blueprints of the stadium. They were also being trained aggressively to take on Dawood and his men without any effective weaponry. The warring team was only months away from tasting success when my darkest fears were realised ...

I learned that one of Sapna's men had squealed to Dawood's right-hand man Chhota Shakeel about her plan. This meant that things could turn extremely dangerous for her. My ego wouldn't allow me to reveal what I'd learned to her, so I started keeping a watch on her whereabouts and also kept myself updated on all the developments in the underworld, because knowing Shakeel's temperament, he was not among those who would keep quiet after hearing about Sapna's daring plan. He had a bad temper and was known to react violently. In this case, I felt, he might not do anything because Sapna was a woman and, up until then, the mafiosi had followed a rigid code of not hurting women or children. I thought that all Dawood's men would do was threaten her with dire consequences. But I was very wrong.

Sapna had recently moved to a small house in Hujjrah Mohalla in Nagpada. Hujrah Mohalla housed small-time goons and was also popular in Dongri for its clothing stores selling readymade garments for women and children. Till around 7 p.m. the lane is usually bustling with commercial activity; after 8, the shopkeepers wrap up for the day and it becomes a den for goondas. They gamble, they plot robberies, pick-pocketing schemes or talk politics and religion. It is the most interesting place to be in at this hour. The reason why Sapna moved there, though, was because it was barely a few metres away from Mussafir Khana, Dawood's paternal home. Sapna had deliberately housed herself close to her enemy's den, so that she could be alerted on movement of any kind. Shifting base closer to the serpent was a bold decision; it was a risky move, something I wouldn't have considered doing.

On that particular night in 1994, Sapna was down with high fever. She asked her men to leave her alone so that she could get some rest. I am sure one of her own goons must have alerted Shakeel to the fact that she would be alone that night.

It was a little before 10 p.m., and Hujjrah Mohalla was bustling. The noisy lane, however, seemed to take a collective breath and stiffen when a red Maruti van drove into the lane. Passers-by saw four men step out of the van with daggers and pistols and force their way into the building where Sapna lived. Before anyone could even react, the men had barged into her house.

Sapna, who I believe was fast asleep on her bed, was completely unprepared. They woke her up and dragged her down onto the floor and began kicking her in the stomach and on the hands first, in order to prevent her from getting hold of any weapon.

Defenceless, Sapna kept screaming for help, but her timid and unarmed neighbours stayed away. By now, the four cowards had reached for their daggers and had begun stabbing her. Instead of killing her at one go, they decided to put her through an extreme level of torture. Perhaps they had been instructed to make her an example for anyone who dared to even think of taking on Dawood. Sapna's flesh was riddled with wounds and blood splattered on the floor. The men deliberately targeted her breasts and vagina, where she suffered over twenty-two stab wounds.

When she had finally collapsed, the four men left the way they had come. The people who had gathered outside the building, drawn there by Sapna's screams, stood by in silence. They all knew that these were Dawood and Shakeel's men and kept away.

When Ahmed told me about what had happened to Sapna, I was shocked. I rushed to the hospital but was told that she had succumbed to her wounds and been brought in dead. My Sapna had gone away in a whiff, and I hadn't been able to do anything.

It's been four years since the incident and I am sure of one thing—Chhota Shakeel and his men will never be brought to book for Ashraf's murder. During the initial investigations, I heard the police had made a few arrests, but they were unable to convict anyone for the crime.

Today, the residents of Hujjrah Mohalla, many of whom were witnesses to the murder, don't even dare to speak about that incident. They are probably trying to forget it ever happened. But I am not like the others. I cannot forget Ashraf because she is the only woman I've ever been so madly besotted with. She made me think and behave like a human being, treating me like a friend and not like a gangster.

I feel responsible for everything that happened to her, and regret turning her into Sapna didi. I knew that her chances to kill Dawood were slim. If I had, without being overcome by her and my own emotions, put some sense into her, she would probably have remained Ashraf, the

Ashraf I knew—a beautiful, burqa-clad Muslim girl. The Ashraf I saw on that day we first met looked like a wilted flower yet her innocence melted me, and her determination astounded me.

I did not realise when Ashraf became Sapna. She, unlike Ashraf, was not ashamed of how the world perceived her. She had lost faith in religion and sought only within herself the strength to avenge her husband's death. Sapna was a woman who wasn't willing to compromise with her emotions. She was magnetic, powerful and painfully attractive, just like a dream, a dream I wasn't ever able to understand.

Sapna was famous, while Ashraf was just another woman. This is why I first mentioned Sapna to you both, because I thought you would have heard about her.

Today, she has made of me what she became after her husband's murder. Yes, I have promised revenge. I won't spare Dawood or Shakeel. I have more reason to destroy them now. I want to see her dream fulfilled through my own hands.

~

When we finally get up to leave, Ustara leads us to the door. 'It was nice meeting you, write something good about me. I am tired of bad publicity,' he says.

Vikram laughs. 'Yes, you are an interesting man after all, with many interesting tales.'

'Of course, my life has been an adventure.'

We are barely out the door when I stop and ask if he has a photograph of Sapna.

Ustara looks at me suspiciously for a moment or two, and then, pointing at his heart, he says, 'I carry this dream in my heart. She is here ... isn't she beautiful?'

EPILOGUE

Mohammad Hussain Shaikh alias Ustara could not fulfil his promise of avenging Ashraf's brutal death. Ustara was one of the most sophisticated gunmen in the Mumbai mafia, and was at all times flanked by half-a- dozen excellent sharpshooters. But Ustara's love for the company of beautiful women inevitably paved the way for his end. Often, the mad surge of lust made him reckless and negligent.

He liked to keep his flings discreet, so Ustara avoided taking his men on his visits to women. What he failed to take into account was that his rivals were not oblivious to his movements, as also his decision to take them on. Chhota Shakeel had set a chain of spies on Ustara. The plan was simple: to wait for an opportunity to strike when Ustara was off guard.

On the evening of 11 September 1998, Ustara asked his men not to follow him. He took his guns and drove out in a grey DCM Daewoo Cielo from his den in Bapurao Pathe Marg. As he reached his girlfriend's house near

Nagpada, the message was relayed to Shakeel in Karachi, who immediately asked his men to assemble and ambush Ustara. Within an hour, the men had taken their positions.

When Ustara exited the building, eyewitnesses later recounted, he didn't look around but headed straight towards his car. The men who were waiting for him decided that this was their moment. Eight men whipped out their guns and showered a volley of bullets on Ustara. It is not known how many rounds were fired but over twenty rounds mowed Ustara down and the rest punched holes in his car. It was over in a matter of seconds. Ustara neither had time to see his assailants nor could he draw his own favourite German Mauser. Ironically, Ustara had been proud of his ability to cock the gun and fire in three seconds.

The cops later filed a report that eight men were seen firing bullets at Ustara. Four of them had come on two bikes, two had come on a scooter and two in a Maruti van. In a rare occurrence in a gangland shootout, an AK-47 was used to kill Ustara. It seemed the men were armed to the teeth, indicating that even if Ustara had managed to put up a fight, he would have had no chance of surviving the attack.

Ustara was rushed to J.J. Hospital where he was declared dead on admission.

FOUR

THE NARCO EMPRESS

Chapter 1

DRUG BARONNESS OF REAY ROAD

Sonapur Lane, also called Sonapur Galli, is just a stone's throw away from the Reay Road railway station. Some thousand shanties nestle here, a nesting ground for crime and disease.

The 'sona' in Sonapur is in no way related to 'gold'; it, in fact, refers to 'death' or 'sleep', because of several Muslim graveyards in the vicinity. But, for one woman in this otherwise nondescript residential hub of Mumbai's underbelly, the area did bring gold and untold wealth. Jyoti Adiramalingam, aka Jyoti amma, is the reigning godmother of the area. She is the one who lays down the rules and she alone has the authority to bend them.

According to the dossiers of the Narcotics Control Bureau and the Anti-Narcotics Cell, Jyoti is one of the many small yet dominant cogs in the humongous machine of the Rs 1,000-crore drug trafficking industry in Mumbai.

The forty-six-year-old is considered to be one of the most feared drug baronesses.

A Sunday cover story on the role of women in the narco- industry took me to Sonapur Galli. Jyoti was fresh out of prison at the time, after having served a four-and-a-half year sentence in Mumbai's Byculla Women's Jail.

On entering the lane, I saw a long line of similar-looking shanties abutting each other. The huts were made of plywood and asbestos sheets, and roofed with tarpaulin covers and plastic sheets. I knew that Jyoti lived in Room No. 70. Oddly, though, most huts in the lane seemed to have No. 70 painted on their doors. I discovered later that this was a ploy to confuse the police so the godmother would have time to escape.

Meanwhile, I had to track down the real No. 70. I was looking around for someone to guide me to Jyoti when I felt a heavy hand on my back. I turned to confront a female version of the Incredible Hulk staring straight at me.

The woman was wearing a pale-coloured sari and was gigantic, with beefy hands. Her ears were adorned with several pairs of diamond earrings, her arms with thick gold bangles, and her neck with chains. The feature that struck me most, though, was her eyebrows, which met below a huge circular red bindi.

It took me a few seconds to realise I was standing in front of Jyoti.

I was suddenly a little nervous; I recalled rumours I'd heard about her beating up a constable at the sessions court during the hearing of one of her drug-peddling cases. It was Jyoti who finally broke the silence. 'Kaun hai tu? Kya mangta hain?' (Who are you? What do you want?)

I clutched my handbag and took a deep breath to ease the feeling of fear that had overtaken me.

'I am a social worker,' I lied, knowing she wouldn't talk to me if I told her I was a journalist. 'I need five to ten minutes of your time. Can we talk here or ...?' I replied in Hindi. Her cold blood-shot eyes looked straight into me and she sized me up. After what seemed like an eternity, she nonchalantly said, 'Come home.'

I followed her as she led me to her shanty. A thin curtain served as a door in her one-storey wooden shack. The room we walked into was dark with hardly any furniture barring a bed, a television set and a fridge. There was no one else in the room. Jyoti offered me a stool and proceeded to sprawl on the bed, which creaked under her weight.

'I am preparing a report on women who have been tortured and harassed by the police ...' I began tentatively.

'Hmm ... So what do you want to know?' she snapped.

'About your business ...'

'Why is a social worker interested in what I do?' she interjected almost immediately.

I squirmed a little in my seat, while trying to prepare a convincing answer.

'I've heard that you used to deal with drugs, due to which you were arrested on several occasions. Has the police ever harassed you during this time?'

'Have you met other women who have been subject to police harassment?'

I realised that while I had come here to ferret information from her, Jyoti was subtly extracting information about me with a barrage of counter-questions. This was going to be more difficult than I'd thought.

'I have interviewed three to four women. Their case has already been taken forward,' I said.

A blanket of unnerving silence followed, which to my relief, was broken by the chugging of a train as it hurtled passed the Reay Road railway station in the vicinity.

'Did you really deal in drugs?' I continued, trying to elicit some response.

She looked at me for a few seconds and then finally answered.

'I became a drug peddler to feed my six children. My husband was unemployed and would drink every day. I needed the money to raise my children. But I stopped it long ago. Now I make idlis and dosas for a living.'

It was hard to imagine any idli-dosa seller being able to deck herself with so much gold.

'But according to the cops, you still sell drugs?'

'Those cops are bloody liars,' she snarled. 'Small fry like us always get convicted but big sharks manage to dodge the law and remain elusive. They outsmart the whole judicial machinery,' she said.

'This means that there is someone bigger than you ...'

'Who said I am big? The real godmother is still

unreachable. The law hasn't been able to convict her and the prosecution hasn't been able to put her behind bars.'

'Who is she?' I asked.

'Why do you want to know?'

'So that our NGO can help her out too ...'

Jyoti grinned and in a mocking tone, said, 'She doesn't need your help. Go to her if *you* ever need any favours.'

'She seems influential.'

'Yes, the Tamil community at Sion Koliwada reveres her. She is named after our goddess.'

'What is her name?' I tried prodding her one last time.

She darted a cold stare at me. 'Bacchi, you ask too many questions.'

For some reason, I was unflustered by her daunting demeanour; my curiosity was getting the better of me.

Durga, Parvati, Saraswati, Lakshmi, Devi ... the names ran through my head.

'Is it Parvati?' I hazarded a guess.

Jyoti grinned and pointed with her fat fingers to a framed picture of a goddess that hung just above the television set. The goddess was draped in a red sari and had four hands.

'Mahalaxmi,' she said.

Beyond this, she refused to divulge any more information on this mystery woman. On my way out, I spotted Jyoti's eldest daughter Asha Tamilsaran Yadav, who had been eavesdropping on our conversation. I had met her two weeks back at the police station. It was she who had given me Jyoti's address. According to the police dossiers, after two decades of successful drug-pushing, Jyoti had handed over the reigns of her business to her twenty-five-year-old daughter Asha.

'Who was your mother talking about?' I asked.

'Mahalaxmi Papamani,' she replied.

Chapter 2

POLITE PRESSURE

A loud thud on the door roused him from his Sunday siesta. Disoriented, he lifted his head and looked at the wall clock. It was 3.30 p.m. Thinking he might have imagined the sound, he dug his face back into the pillow but a second later, the banging started again, and this time it didn't stop. He hurriedly scrambled out of his bed, to find his main door shaking from the force with which it was being knocked on.

'Who is it?' he asked brusquely.

There was no response from the other end but the banging continued.

'Wait, wait, I'm coming. Be patient.' His head was still heavy, so he ran into his bathroom, splashed some cold water on his face and rushed back to open the door. Since the Hindu–Muslim riots and the subsequent serial blasts in Mumbai, the mood in the city had been tense. Was it bad news, he wondered as he unlocked the door. He took a step back immediately. Before him stood about thirty men, all dressed in shirts and lungis.

He rushed back inside his one-room tenement and towards the window to call for help, only to stop short. A large number of men and women were squatting on the footpath opposite his building and staring right at his home. Before he could move, the entire pack of men in the passageway had entered his house. He suddenly felt powerless and began sweating. He quickly scanned the men in front of him to check if they were carrying any weapons. To his relief, none of them seemed to have anything with them. Why were they here? What did they want? As a prominent lawyer in Mumbai's legal circuit, with a good number of successful narco trials at the very onset of his career, Ayaz Khan was a source of envy for his colleagues and enemies alike. Several had been eager to see his flourishing career quashed. Ayaz now began to wonder if these people were there at the behest of one of his enemies.

'What is all this?' he asked the men, the fear audible in his voice.

'Amma ko police uthake le gayi (The police has picked up our mother),' one of them said, in accented Hindi.

'Kiski amma? (Whose mother),' he asked, taken aback.

'Hum sabki amma (All of ours),' the same man responded and shoved some papers in his hand. He seemed to be the leader of the group.

Ayaz calmly handed back the papers. 'See, I don't entertain people at my home. Come to the court tomorrow,' he said.

'We won't harm you. Just take up Amma's case,' one of them said, sensing Ayaz's irritation.

'The court is shut. I cannot do anything today.'

'We only need an answer.'

'First, get all your men out of here. I don't want any tamasha. I will only speak to one man.'

Surprisingly, the leader of the group agreed at once. He spoke to his men in a language that Ayaz presumed was Tamil. Within a few minutes, everybody except for the leader had quietly disappeared from his home.

'We know that you can help us. Amma wants you to fight her case. Don't bother about the money, Amma has lots,' the man said.

'I will need all the details.'

The man handed Ayaz the stack of papers once again. Ayaz scanned through it briefly. 'Get these papers and come to the court at 10 tomorrow morning.'

'Thank you, saar. Amma will bless you,' the man said, and fell at Ayaz's feet.

Ayaz stepped back. 'No, please don't do all this. Just one request, don't get all these men to court. Otherwise I won't be able to get your Amma out.'

The man nodded and left.

Ayaz was at the sessions court early the next day. As a specialist in narcotics-related cases, he had heard a lot about Mahalaxmi Papamani through both his colleagues and the cops. She had been in the news on more than one occasion. For someone who had started off as a small-time peddler, Papamani had acquired quite a notorious reputation in Mumbai's drug scene. Ayaz couldn't wait to share the experience of his first brush with the Papamani menace with his lawyer friends.

The sessions court building in Kalaghoda, home to hundreds of lawyers and paralegals, comprises several civil and criminal courtrooms connected by labyrinthine alleys and rows of stairs. Ayaz had reached the first floor when three women stopped him. They were dressed in gaudy saris and had red and yellow bindis on their foreheads.

'Saar, Mahalaxmi Papamani's case ...'

'Oh, yes,' Ayaz said, not the least surprised. 'Where is the man who came to my house yesterday?' he asked sarcastically.

'He doesn't handle court-related work. Amma has chosen us as her advisors. We know the law and will guide you in this case.'

Ayaz couldn't hold back a smile. 'No, don't bother. Give me the papers and I will handle everything.'

But the women didn't move; instead they made Ayaz sit down and hear them out. Twenty minutes into the conversation, Ayaz had learnt his lesson: appearances could be deceptive. These women were actually well-read legal functionaries of Papamani. They knew the Narcotics Drugs and Psychotropic Substances Act by rote. In fact, they actually enlightened Ayaz about the technical loopholes in the prosecution's case. Even before meeting her, Ayaz was impressed with the team of brain and brawn that Papamani had gathered around her.

Later that afternoon, the women took Ayaz to the Anti- Narcotics Cell lock-up, located inside the Esplanade Court compound, to meet Mahalaxmi. The compound—which also houses the Azad Maidan police station—is always bustling with lawyers, policemen, criminals and media persons. The small lock-up faces the outside and passers- by can look in.

When Ayaz reached the ANC office, he could not resist throwing a glance at the lock-up. He wanted to get his first glimpse of the woman who had such clout over the lower echelons of Tamil society in Mumbai.

'Where is Mahalaxmi?' he asked the women who had accompanied him.

The shortest among the three pointed out to a swarthy woman, sitting stoically on a wooden stool. A young girl stood beside her, fanning her with a newspaper, while an old woman pressed her legs. Even though she was behind bars, there was a serene and unflustered expression on her face.

'Amma,' one of the women who had come with Ayaz called out.

On hearing the familiar voice, she turned towards them. And then shifted her gaze to Ayaz, the lawyer who would be fighting her case.

Chapter 3

FROM RAGS TO RICHES

Mahalaxmi Papamani—the wealthiest drug baroness in Mumbai and revered by Tamilians from the lower classes—had very humble beginnings. She was the daughter of a labourer and construction worker from the Salem district of Tamil Nadu.

Born to Periaswamy and Meenakshi in 1960, Papamani spent most of her childhood in a slum on Shivaji Road in Bangalore, along with her three siblings, Naathan, Mohan and Yashoda. Given that the family lived hand-to-mouth, none of the four children was able to receive an education.

In 1980, Papamani relocated to Mumbai. Apparently the relocation was part of Tamilian don Vardharajan Muniswami Mudaliar's plan to build a mini-Tamil Nadu in Mumbai. Vardharajan, or Vardha bhai as he was known, owned an illicit hooch liquor distillery (khaadi) at Sion-Koliwada in central Mumbai. He had quite a following among south Indians, having brought hordes of men from the poverty-stricken regions of Salem to work in his khaadi, even as the women were employed in red-light areas. Over several years, the Tamilians started settling in makeshift homes around Sion-Koliwada and, consequently, the slum came into being. Papamani became one of Vardha's most favoured companions. Because of her proximity to the don, men and women in the Sion-Koliwada area treated her with respect.

However, with prohibition being lifted in the '80s and the simultaneous decline of Vardharajan, Papamani's fortunes plummeted. The same people who once looked at her with awe now turned their backs on her.

With no one to consider as family, Papamani was suddenly left to fend for herself. However, her determination to survive helped her rise again. She started off as a rag-picker and then took to working as a domestic help in the Antop Hill neighbourhood until she met Mani Chinapayya Devendra, who allegedly peddled drugs before he started working as a helper in an edible oil company in Sewree.

Papamani got married to Devendra and began living with her in-laws at a slum in suburban Mumbai near Mankhurd station. After shifting from one shanty to another, the couple finally bought a small room near the Hanuman Temple at the Sion-Koliwada slum in Antop Hill.

In the years that followed, she had four daughters and one son with Devendra: Jayanti, Lalita, Jayshree, Jayalaxmi and Venkatesh.

However, life had another setback in store for Papamani. Her husband, an alcoholic, spent most of his money getting drunk in the evenings. During one of his drunken stints, he met with an accident that left him paralysed for life. With five children to raise and a disabled, unemployed husband at home, Papamani was forced to hunt for a new source of income.

It was during these troubled times that she was approached by her neighbour and friend, Savitri, a prominent drug peddler in the Sion-Koliwada slum. Savitri sold pudis (packets) of heroin. Since the drug-peddling business was highly profitable, Papamani immediately decided to give it a shot. Savitri also lured Jyoti Adiramalingam from Reay Road, to work for her. Under Savitri's tutelage, Papamani and Jyoti were given the responsibility of dividing large quantities of heroin into smaller pudis and then distributing them to interested parties.

In no time, the troika of women—Savitri, Papamani and Jyoti—had begun to control the pudi-selling business in Sion-Koliwada. However, with profits running into lakhs, it was only a matter of time before Papamani outsmarted her own mentor, with her shrewd, business acumen.

In 1991, Papamani decided to split from Savitri and began running the business independently with the help of a loyal group of peddlers. Papamani's business strategy was simple. She would buy five kilogrammes of heroin at anywhere between one to three lakh rupees and would then convert ten grams of heroin into forty pudis. She then sold each pudi at twenty-five rupees, making a profit of around three lakh rupees per month, i.e. about the salary of a CEO of a company in Mumbai. Sometimes, she would also peddle large quantities of heroin for regular customers. The police tried to arrest her on several occasions but she always managed to escape conviction, for want of evidence.

In the months that followed, the coterie of people working for her tripled, and this illiterate slum-dweller soon went on to launch a full-fledged empire with her own financial managers, peddlers and advisors, literally converting the Sion-Koliwada slum into a drug den.

Papamani also engaged several hundreds of unemployed men and women in the drug-peddling business, providing a source of income to the many deprived families of Sion-Koliwada. She had begun to make so much money, she was forced to stock liquid cash in several hutments across the slum. With crores of rupees always at her disposal, her involvement in charity work also began to increase. She was considered the poor man's bank, as she would loan people money to run their households. It is said that Papamani kept thirty to forty lakh rupees in cash tucked inside her sari and fearlessly walked the narrow alleys of her slum area, distributing money to poor Tamilians in return for their services.

Her charity work did not deter her from multiplying her own finances. And so, even while she continued to live in her small shanty, she began investing money in lucrative businesses. Her first destination for investment was

Bangalore. Despite having made her money in Mumbai, Papamani still had a soft spot for the city in which she had spent her childhood. It was here that she allegedly started a three-star hotel. She also bought herself a house and four shops in Trichy, in the Salem district. Papamani gave all these shops on rent and employed someone to collect the rent from the tenants.

Soon, because of her role in transforming the poverty-stricken Sion-Koliwada slum into a place of wealth, the locals christened her Mahalaxmi, the Hindu goddess of wealth. Papamani was now Mahalaxmi Papamani Chinapayya Devendra.

Then, in 1993, the Mumbai police's Anti-Narcotics Cell (ANC) arrested her once again. This time, the ANC was confident about throwing her in jail for a very long time. Papamani knew she was in trouble, and in an urgent bid to secure release, she roped in narco-specialist Ayaz Khan. She knew that if there was any lawyer who could get her out of prison, it was Ayaz. Her faith was not misplaced: Ayaz successfully managed to spot loopholes in the ANC's case, and Papamani was released on bail.

~

Papamani's popularity and support within Sion-Koliwada was apparent also from the way the slum-dwellers took personal interest in shielding her. For instance, escape routes were charted within the slum. The Sion-Koliwada slum is built on the slope of a hill and the shanties are attached to each other. The path leading to these shanties is also narrow and maze-like. To help her escape, the slum-dwellers created several routes, hideouts and underground passageways within the connected hutments. These routes eventually led outside the slum. Every time the police came to arrest Papamani, people in the slum would be warned and she would be sent out through one of these routes.

Matters became more complicated when Papamani came up with a novel idea to escape arrests. Several times, the police would be confronted with an impenetrable wall of eunuchs, who formed a human barricade for the entire stretch of the slum. These eunuchs were much stronger and abusive than the locals, and the cops usually avoided any confrontation with them.

An officer with the Narcotics Control Bureau (NCB), who was personally involved in Papamani's arrest in 2004, narrated how Papamani's army of eunuchs accosted them when the cops nabbed her. They surrounded the officer's jeep in which Papamani had been herded and stopped it from moving ahead, demanding that Papamani be freed. After much difficulty and a lathi-charge by the Antop Hill police, the officer managed to escape from the slum with Papamani in the car.

~

Papamani soon separated from her husband Devendra, leaving him to fend for himself. Reluctant to get any of her children involved in her line of work, she sent four of them to study at the elite JR Cambridge boarding school in Salem. Her children though, were not interested in studies, and after they failed repeatedly in school, Papamani finally had to bring all of them back to Mumbai, four years later. She got three of her daughters married in Mumbai; one married the son of Papamani's mentor, Savitri.

At around the same time, her twenty-year-old daughter Jayshree, who was a Class 9 dropout, started having an affair with a local ruffian, Vijay Gupta. Their relationship caused Papamani a lot of embarrassment, partly because the boy was from a different caste and partly because he was a local goon, and she was thought of highly by the locals.

In her confessional statement to the NCB, Papamani admitted that, since she was preoccupied with the heroin business and occasionally absconding to evade arrests, she could not pay attention to Jayshree. Papamani finally filed a case of molestation against Gupta and sent her daughter to a distant relative's place. But all her attempts to shelter Jayshree went in vain, as the girl continued her affair. Assuming that her daughter was already 'spoilt', Papamani decided to make Jayshree her successor. Jayshree was initially roped in to sell pudis and then gradually made to deliver bigger consignments to Papamani's clients.

On the afternoon of 19 July 2004, the NCB caught Jayshree with four kilos of heroin. Papamani was eventually arrested around ten days later.

Investigations revealed that Papamani had connections with NCB's most prized catch, Ghasiram Solanki, who was one of the leading drug traffickers in India. However, Papamani maintained that she did not know him personally. She said that, while she was on the run, she had stayed in the house of a friend Laxmi Karpai, who bought heroin in large quantities from a woman known as Hamida aka Aapa. Hamida, she said, used to arrange for the heroin from Solanki.

The NCB had been looking for evidence and witnesses against Papamani. To their luck, Papamani's husband Devendra, who all this while had been holding a grudge against her for what he saw as her abandoning him, decided to stand witness against her.

During his testimony, Devendra revealed information about some of Papamani's prime properties in Salem and Mumbai, which she had bought with the income she earned from the sale of heroin. 'My wife is in the heroin business and I am not on good terms with her,' Devendra said. Jayshree, who was also upset with her mother's attempts to keep her away from her lover and force her into the drug trade, also decided to stand witness against her.

Papamani was finally convicted and put behind bars in 2004. It was ironic that the two people for whom Papamani earned turned against her. While she had so many followers, none of them were in her family.

Knowing perhaps, that Papamani's influence would extend beyond the jail she was in, not one of the residents of Sion-Koliwada had stood witness against her. Her husband had, and he paid for it with his life.

In 2007, Devendra was murdered under mysterious circumstances. For the record, he was killed by a group of drug addicts and thrown onto the railway tracks. But neighbours believe that his fate was sealed the day he decided to act against his wife.

Papamani was released two years after her arrest. These two years of confinement marked the worst phase in her life. Her fortunes took a nosedive as all her benami properties were seized by the NCB and the Mumbai police. After Devendra's death, Papamani's heir-apparent Jayshree eloped with another local ruffian. From being a crorepati, Papamani was now scraping loose change.

Chapter 4

ENCOUNTER WITH THE EMPRESS

The grey Tata Safari halted at one corner of Antop Hill's busy market area. I got down and started walking towards the junction. The street was dotted with shanties, small vegetable and fruit stalls, tea and second- hand furniture shops. The market was bustling with people and everyone, right from the vendors to the locals, seemed to be conversing in Tamil. It is the local language in the area, and though I was in central Mumbai, I could well have been in some small town in Tamil Nadu.

This is the Sion-Koliwada slum, infamous for its illicit hooch distillery owned by Vardharajan in the '80s, and later, notorious for being a drug den under Mahalaxmi Papamani. While most of the residents of the slum may have found other sources of income today, there are several whose lives suffered irreversible damage as a result of these little industries. The slum is built on a hill that leads to a Hindu temple. These hutments reminded me of the ones I had seen at Sonapur Lane in Reay Road when I met Jyoti Adiramlingam. I was told that Papamani still lived here.

Since she was known to all, I assumed that it would be easy to locate her. I was wrong. Most of the people in the area refused to acknowledge her existence, let alone speak about her goddess-like aura.

After receiving vague replies, suspicious glares and misleading directions from several people, I decided to approach a woman who, I'd noticed, had been spying on me while I moved around asking for Mahalaxmi's whereabouts.

'What do you know about Papamani?' she growled.

'She is the Amma out here,' I said, choosing my words carefully.

'What if I told you I am Papamani?' she asked mockingly.

I had seen Papamani in the photographs that I had procured from the NCB dossiers and the woman in front of me looked nothing like her.

'No, you aren't,' I said politely.

She immediately broke into a sardonic smile. 'She sits at that junction,' she said, pointing to the junction ahead.

I expressed my thanks to her with an awkward smile and began walking. I must have gone a little beyond the junction, when I became conscious of a woman who had been sitting all alone near a wooden cart.

'Are you looking for me?' she called out, in heavily accented Hindi.

I turned around, and was stunned.

She was Papa (God help me) Mani. Papamani. Mahalaxmi Papamani. My jaw dropped on seeing her.

The woman whom I had only known by reputation or police and NCB dossiers, was actually right in front of me, sitting calmly, fanning herself with the pallu of her black saree. I thought I would never be able to trace her but it almost seemed like she had been anticipating my arrival.

I was surprised that she did not have her gang of eunuchs or coterie around.

'Why did you want to meet me?' she asked, as I came closer.

'I am a social worker,' I lied, just as I had to Jyoti.

'I am self-sufficient. I don't need your help.'

'We can find you work,' I persisted.

'Me? I already have a lot of work,' she interrupted, pointing to the wooden cart in front of her. 'Look here, this is my livelihood. I make enough from this.'

I looked at the cart and saw that there was a heap of onions and potatoes on it.

'I sell vegetables. Do you want some?' she asked sarcastically.

For a brief moment, I did not know how to react, but I was desperate to continue the conversation. 'Yes, two kilos each,' I replied hurriedly.

Papamani was taken aback; she hadn't expected me to actually buy the vegetables. She quickly recovered though, and as she began placing the vegetables on a weighing scale, I asked, 'Since when have you been doing this?'

'Two years,' she replied.

'What about the police cases against you then?'

'Police cases?'

'For selling drugs ...'

'The police is envious of me. My dhanda helped sustain thousands of families in Sion-Koliwada. The hungry were fed with my money while the poor got their children educated. I was doing good work for society.'

'Then why did you open this vegetable stall?'

'My husband is dead; my daughter ran away. I did not see a reason to make so much money anymore,' she said, as she put the vegetables in a black plastic bag. 'Forty-five rupees.'

I promptly paid her.

As she counted the money, I was reminded of the stories of Papamani distributing lakhs of rupees to people. The four crisp ten rupee notes and the five rupee coin that I handed to her were nowhere near the kind of money she had handled in the past. Satisfied after counting the money, she nodded at someone on the opposite end of the road. It was then that I noticed the people around us, watching us talk. I ignored them and tried to get her to speak again.

'I can still help you if you want me to.'

'Give me fifty thousand rupees,' she demanded out of nowhere.

'For?'

'I need it for an operation. It can save my life.'

'I don't have that kind of money now.'

'Get it, and then we can continue talking.'

Her proposition shocked me; it sounded like extortion to me. But the situation became even more uncomfortable when I noticed that a group of five to six menacing-looking Tamil women had begun encircling the stall. Sensing something was amiss, I decided to make a move. I quickly took the two polythene bags and walked away quietly.

'Keep buying from here,' Papamani said with a smile.

I nodded, although I wasn't sure whether she meant the potatoes and onions or the pudis, the business, which like Jyoti, she claimed to have stopped long ago. I walked away and, when I felt there was enough distance between me and the women, I turned around to look at Papamani for one last time.

She was not sitting near the junction anymore. As for the vegetable stall, I saw a young boy stuff the vegetables into a jute bag and leave. In a few minutes, the place had been cleared. I got into the Safari, still in a quandary about the pieces of this Papamani jigsaw puzzle. Something was just not right. But I was glad that I had walked away unharmed from the place.

A few days after the incident, I got a call from an informant, who claimed to have helped the NCB arrest Papamani.

'I heard you met Papamani,' he said.

'How did you know?' I asked, astonished.

'It's a much talked-about setup at Sion-Koliwada,' he replied with nonchalance.

'What setup? What do you mean?' I asked incredulously.

'All that you saw was staged to trick you. It was a farce for your benefit.'

The revelation stunned me, but at least now the puzzle was complete. The whole decoy was intended to throw me off track. The reality of Papamani was far from what I had seen of her at the vegetable market.

FIVE

MOBSTER'S MOLL

Chapter 1

THE FLIGHT FROM LISBON

The police convoy cut across the runway, its blaring sirens not raising even one eyebrow amidst the din at Lisbon airport. The gun-toting guards accompanying the convoy gave the impression of it being a mobile fortress. The cars screeched to a halt and officers of the Policia Judicia stepped out, escorting a thirty-six-year-old man, dressed in a black T-shirt and track pants. He had a stooping gait and seemed to be smiling nervously. The Portuguese police spoke to him before he was taken over to the eagerly waiting contingent of Indian officials.

For a moment, deputy superintendent of police, Special Task Force, CBI Devendra Pardesi, couldn't believe his eyes. He had handled tough cases and tougher criminals, but this one seemed a bit unreal. The man the Portuguese police was handing over just didn't fit the bill of one of Mumbai's most dreaded gangsters—someone who had masterminded some of the most gruesome murders in the annals of Mumbai crime history.

Pardesi had barely collected his thoughts when the occupant of the second car stepped out. Just as in the movies, a policeman held the door open as a woman's legs emerged from the vehicle and daintily settled on the tarmac, toes first and then the heels as she climbed gracefully out of the car. Her fair skin appeared pale and almost translucent in the afternoon heat. Tall and slim, she had very delicate features that were strained at the moment as she clutched a Bible like it was a lifesaver. Her long, thin legs and narrow waistline were emphasised in the figure- hugging T-shirt and jeans that she wore.

Monica Bedi was no Madhuri Dixit but she was attractive—Pardesi thought she fit the bill of a mobster's moll perfectly. He wondered how this otherwise naïve-looking woman could have gotten involved in such a mess. His boss, deputy inspector general of police, CBI, Omprakash Chhatwal, signed the official documents and nodded at Pardesi, who moved cautiously towards Abu Salem.

'So, you are Salem?' Pardesi asked.

'Are you from the Crime Branch?' Salem's voice betrayed fear.

'No, we are from the CBI,' Pardesi replied.

Salem seemed to relax when he heard this. 'Then, saab, let's leave for our country.'

The motley group began walking towards the huge

Russian-made cargo plane of the Indian Air Force that was waiting for them on the tarmac. The CBI had finally managed to get Salem and Monica on a flight to Mumbai.

The entire mission to bring Salem and Monica back from Lisbon to Mumbai had been a secret operation. The CBI agents were apprehensive of any political pressure that might be exerted to obstruct their plans. When it came to secrets, the Parliament was the leakiest ship in the country.

Further, Monica—after an interview with a local channel—had managed to create a huge sympathy wave among the Portuguese, especially nuns. During her three years in a Lisbon jail, public opinion had shifted in her favour, and any move against her might have provoked the locals and proved detrimental to the Portuguese government.

While planning how to get the don and Monica Bedi back to India, the CBI had decided against a civilian aircraft, and opted for a cargo plane instead. The plane they were embarking now was just a box with wings. Once you entered its wide body, you found yourself in a massive open space with one line of metallic benches fitted on each side. There were ropes hanging from the ceiling and also a mini crane at the far end, near the cargo hold. The plane had a urinal, but no decent commode.

Both Salem and Monica seemed to be visibly affected by the sight of the plane that would take them back home to a posse of policemen and hordes of journalists. The bleakness seemed to portend their future and the duo looked disturbed. Once inside the plane, Pardesi handcuffed Salem to one bench, to prevent any attempts the don might make to hurt himself. If anything happened to Salem en route, human rights activists would haul them over the coals.

'Saab, can I meet Monica for one last time?' Salem pleaded. A thick curtain separated the two.

'Don't you dare move from where you are,' Pardesi said, glaring at him.

The behemoth revved up its engine and, with an ear-splitting roar, began taxiing for takeoff. The couple had no view of the country they were leaving behind.

On the other side of the curtain, Monica sat calmly, showing no signs of anxiety or eagerness to speak to anyone on board. She was reading her copy of the Bible when Pardesi went and sat beside her. Monica seemed reluctant to speak to the CBI officer; she clutched her Bible firmly and shut her eyes instead, sinking deep into thought and reminiscences.

~

Monica heaved a sigh of relief as the plane climbed higher and higher. Soon she would be back in Mumbai, the city she had left hurriedly over four years ago. Would the city and its people embrace her again, she wondered. Would her co-stars and friends speak to her? She feared the worst.

After four hours, the plane landed at Cairo International

Airport. Chhatwal and Pardesi disembarked to stretch their legs while the aircraft was being refuelled. Salem was not allowed to move.

After a stopover of two hours, the plane took off for its final destination of Mumbai. The long journey had finally made Salem open up. He chatted with Pardesi, the deafening roar of the engines notwithstanding. He spoke of Monica and his family. On the other side of the curtain, Monica didn't say a word as she read passages from the Bible. At 7.30 a.m., IL-256 landed at the Chhatrapati Shivaji International Airport in Mumbai.

Gangster Abu Salem was finally back in the city that had given him his livelihood when he had landed there from the boondocks of Azamgarh in Uttar Pradesh. The city had brought him notoriety and elevated him to gangster status. Chhatwal and Pardesi were relieved. They had managed to bring Salem and Monica back and successfully carry out the biggest assignment that the duo had been given in their respective careers.

At the airport, the officers were greeted by Intelligence Bureau agents who took Salem along with them for a brief grilling session. Meanwhile, Pardesi took Monica to a waiting room. He would be handing Monica over to the CBI sleuths from Hyderabad, who were expected any moment. Monica was going to be arrested for securing a fake passport from Kurnool in Andhra Pradesh in 2001, under a fictitious name and address. She had already been booked under sections 420, 471 and 468 of the

Indian Penal Code, 13 (2) to be read with 13 (1d) of the Prevention of Corruption Act and 12 (1B) of the Passport Act.

In the room she sat silently, even as Pardesi scanned her documents. She still held on to the Bible firmly. 'Are you Christian?' Pardesi asked her. She nodded. Pardesi observed her carefully. He couldn't stop wondering how a beautiful starlet had landed up with an uncouth and cold-blooded gangster like Salem.

'I am curious ...' he said after a few minutes of silence. Monica looked at him, and he continued, 'You knew that he was a wanted gangster ... a ruthless murderer with blood on his hands. And yet, you decided to stick with him. Why?'

'It was a mistake. I made the mistake of falling in love with him,' is all she said, and then she broke down.

Chapter 2

BOLLYWOOD DREAMS

That one phone call changed my life.

My career was finally taking off and I was revelling in my new-found success. After struggling for nearly a decade, I had finally managed to get a break in A-grade Bollywood films like *Jaanam Samjha Karo, Jodi No.1* and *Pyaar, Ishq aur Mohabbat*. Romancing actors like Salman Khan, Sanjay Dutt and Arjun Rampal onscreen meant that I had arrived and had opened the floodgates to new offers from reputed filmmakers.

Everything seemed to be going perfectly, just like a fairy tale, until that one phone call.

'Take the first flight to Dubai, because you are in big trouble,' he told me.

Without weighing the implications of what he'd said, I hurriedly arranged for a ticket, packed my bags and rushed to the airport. Fortunately, I had no assignments or shoots lined up, so I could leave in peace. Despite his words, I wasn't overly worried; I didn't really sense anything amiss. At the end of the day, I was going back to the man I loved. A man I loved so much, that it had blinded me to the trouble I was getting myself into.

I walked into the plane and took my seat. People looked at me, recognising me, and I smiled back at them. There was no doubt that they knew who I was. This sort of fame and success hadn't come easily to me. My life is an example of a girl who was born in the back of beyond, and yet rose to fame and success.

I was born to a middle-class Sikh family in a small village in Chabbewal, fifteen kilometres from the town of Hoshiarpur in Punjab on 18 January 1975. My village has seen many of its families migrate to the West. Ten months after I was born, my father Dr Prem Bedi, a practising doctor in Punjab, and my mother, Shakuntala Bedi, decided to migrate to Norway.

In the 1970s, the Indian community in Norway was small, just a few hundred or so of us, which is why we were all very close. In Norway, my father quit his medical practice and started his own garment business in the city of Drammen, forty-five kilometres from Norway's capital, Oslo. As a child, I enjoyed a protected life, free of any worries. My parents too ensured that my brother Bobby and I were never denied anything. The only Hindi films I saw then were on video cassettes that we watched at home.

Then, in 1992, when I was barely seventeen, I decided

to move to England to study English literature. I'd always been a good student but it was a difficult decision for my family because, while I wanted to live independently, my parents were protective and thought I was too young. In the end, I convinced them. England was beautiful and I really began to enjoy the freedom living in a different country gave me. However, I soon knew that this wasn't what I really wanted to do. But since I had persuaded my parents to send me to England, I had no option but to continue.

After studying for a few months in England, I went on a brief holiday to Mumbai. It is then that my life suddenly took a U-turn. I made certain decisions that changed the course of where I was heading. I don't know what drove me into doing what I eventually did but it all started with my meeting with yesteryear Bollywood star Manoj Kumar.

During my stay in Mumbai, I had enrolled at the Gopi Kishan dance classes to learn Kathak. One day, while I was at the class, Manoj-ji happened to drop by. The hero of *Roti, Kapda aur Makaan* and *Upkaar* was a shadow of his former self, but his magnetic charm still lingered.

Manoj-ji spoke endlessly about the Hindi film industry and paid me many compliments. He told me that my face had the perfect blend of the actresses of the'50s and'60s and was the novelty needed for Indian cinema today. Suddenly, I was filled with aspirations to glamour and fame.

After giving it some thought, I called up my parents and told them that I wanted to become an actor. They were reluctant initially and even tried hard to dissuade me. After a lot of dilly-dallying, they finally gave in. However, my decision came at a cost. I had to choose between my studies and a career in Bollywood. I opted for the latter. The glitter of glamour had obfuscated my own judgement. Since I was new to Mumbai my mother shifted base and moved to the city to stay with me. My struggle to find a footing in the Hindi film industry began.

I first got my portfolio made and started off with small assignments. However, the fast-paced life of the city soon began to take a toll on me. The film industry is like a hungry ocean, it takes a lot of effort to stay afloat. Someone told me that, in Bollywood, you either sleep your way to success or hobnob with filmmakers and get acquainted with them. So I began attending 'filmy' events.

I remember going to Bollywood director Subhash Ghai's Holi party. Many aspiring and wannabe actresses would attend such functions, in the hope of meeting film directors and landing small roles in their films. I was raw and had no knowledge about the film industry. During the party, I met Rakesh Roshan. When I was a kid, I had seen some of his films and knew him as an actor; I did not know that he was also a producer and director. At that party, Rakeshji offered me a role opposite Bollywood heartthrob Salman Khan in his forthcoming film *Karan Arjun*. He said that he was looking for a fresh face and was going to start shooting for the movie soon. He also told me that he would like to see me in his office and gave me his phone number and office address. But I began to wonder why an actor would offer me a role. Since I was unsure about his offer, I didn't visit his office and the role eventually went to Mamata Kulkarni. I had missed the opportunity to be launched in a big banner film because of my naïveté and lack of knowledge about the industry.

Capricornian women are said to be strong-willed and ambitious, yet shy and self-contained by nature. I was living proof of this. My biggest problem was that I was embarrassed to go out and ask for work. I didn't have an ego but I couldn't get myself to ask anyone for anything, leave alone a film.

And so, even after struggling for months, I did not have anything on hand. Disappointed, I half-heartedly moved to Hoshiarpur with my mother. However, tragedy struck when a group of bandits attacked my family in Chabbewal, killing my grandparents in the most brutal manner and severely injuring my mother. My mother, who was traumatised by the incident, went to live with her brother in Delhi. She refused to relocate to Norway, even as my extended family moved there. Later, though, after much coaxing, my mother left for Norway.

I chose to come back to Mumbai in 1995. Now I was all on my own and was forced to fend for myself. I couldn't allow my reserved nature to be an obstacle this time. And so I lapped up whatever small or big roles I got. It is during this time that I met film producer Mukesh Duggal, who signed me up for *Suraksha*, starring Saif Ali Khan and

Suniel Shetty. Despite great actors in the lead, the film bombed at the box office.

But I didn't give up. I began doing a lot of films with Duggalji. There were rumours that we were having an affair, which initially disturbed me, but I learned to take these things in my stride. I realised that when you are talked about by the media, it means you have arrived. Unfortunately, Duggalji was shot dead by the underworld in 1997. Once again, I was heartbroken. I had lost my only mentor in Bollywood to the mafia. Little did I know that my fate would soon be linked with the mafia.

Meanwhile, all my films failed to make a mark at the box office. I even tried my hand at Telugu cinema, where I did some quality work and was appreciated, too. I also did some small shows to make ends meet in Mumbai.

Then, one day, I got a call from a businessman in Dubai. He introduced himself as Arsalan Ali and said that he was organising a show, in which he wanted me to perform. I agreed. Arsalan told me that he would get back to me after all the formalities were completed. A few days later, he called me up again. This time, we hit it off and spoke for a really long time. I realised he did not speak English fluently. While I would occasionally break into English, Arsalan did not go beyond a 'hello' or a 'thank you'. I did not have a problem with this because my Hindi wasn't very good either at one point. Soon, the calls became very regular and I, too, started getting more than friendly with him. The strange part is that I hadn't even met him.

It was through our phone calls that I realised that we had a connection.

I really enjoyed speaking to him and would wait anxiously for his calls. I woke up in the morning, anticipating a call from him and went to sleep at night thinking about the conversation we'd had during the day. Suddenly, I had begun to think less about my family and more about him. It was very strange: I hadn't even seen him and I didn't know what he looked like either, yet I was drawn to him.

Over the next few months, we became really close. It was only a matter of time before I knew that I was in love with him. Honestly, I never thought I'd ever fall for a man, merely talking to him over the phone.

We finally met in Dubai and it was beautiful. He proposed to me and I agreed without hesitating. I finally had someone in my life who genuinely loved and cared for me. After this, I visited Dubai once more. When he invited me to come for the third time, I asked him to visit Mumbai instead but he gave me some excuse or the other.

Since Arsalan was a Muslim, I was reluctant to tell my parents the truth about him. Instead, I told them that I was friendly with one 'Sanjay'. They were happy for me.

In the initial days of our relationship, I couldn't really make out what kind of person he was. I would be in Dubai for two or three days only and then I'd return to Mumbai. He was always on his best behaviour during my visits. He was privy to my struggles and he told me that he had good contacts in the film industry and that he would help me get good roles. He was true to his word. Good offers began pouring in quickly. I was first cast as a supporting actor in *Jaanam Samjha Karo* with Salman Khan and Urmila Matondkar. The movie wasn't a super hit but it didn't bomb like my previous films. Over the next two years, I got bigger offers, one from the director of comedies David Dhawan for a lead role opposite Sanjay Dutt in the film *Jodi No. 1*. The movie went on to become a huge box office hit—my first hit. I got another meaty role in director Rajiv Rai's *Pyaar, Ishq aur Mohabbat,* where I was seen wooing upcoming actor Arjun Rampal. I knew that Arsalan may have had something to do with these films, and that he might have wielded his influence in the industry and pulled some strings. Meanwhile, the media tried to deride my success by planting stories of an underworld connection behind all the good roles I was getting. I rebuffed these rumours and didn't think about it too much—I was too overwhelmed by my success. This was the happiest period of my life. I had a wonderful boyfriend and big movies in my kitty. My dreams were close to being realised. And then the phone call came.

~

Arsalan was waiting for me at the Arrivals section at the Dubai International Airport. He looked remorseful and I could sense a lot of tension on his face. He didn't speak much in the car. I asked him why he had asked me to come to Dubai immediately but he sidestepped my questions. It was only when we were at his home that he spoke to me.

'You can never go back to Mumbai,' he told me. For a moment, I was stunned. I had left my clothes, my apartment, my car, *everything* behind because I thought I would be back in two weeks at the most. Now, Arsalan was telling me that I wouldn't be returning to the city of my dreams.

'Why?' I asked.

'The police will force you to reveal my identity,' he told me.

'What do you mean?' I asked him, confused.

This is when Arsalan revealed the truth to me. He told me that his name was Abu Salem and that he was not a businessman from Dubai but a gangster with underworld connections. The police had found out that I was in a relationship with him and he was afraid that they would detain me under some law. Which is why he had asked me to leave Mumbai immediately. I was stunned. Actually, even if he had introduced himself as Abu Salem earlier, I would have had no clue. I had only heard about Dawood Ibrahim and Chhota Shakeel. I had never heard of Abu Salem.

But nothing was as painful as what followed. Salem told me that he was already married to Samira Jumani and that he had a child with her. 'But I only love you and want to start my life afresh with you,' he said. I cried a lot that day. In fact, I had probably never cried as much in my life. Fate had now turned me into nothing more than a mobster's moll.

Chapter 3

THE FUGITIVES

On 11 September 2001, suicide attackers from the Al Qaeda crashed planes into the iconic World Trade Centre towers, shattering the lives of several thousand Americans. There was a growing anti-terror and anti- Islam sentiment in the US, with almost every Muslim in the US fearing for his or her life. Salem and I were among the several anxious south Asian Muslims who witnessed this traumatic phase unfold, after 9/11.

We had escaped from Dubai to the United States just days after the Indian police had learned of my association with Salem. In Dubai, I found out that the CBI had seized my apartment in Mumbai and frozen all my bank accounts. All my escape routes suddenly appeared blocked except for the one that led to Salem.

I was devastated when Salem revealed his real identity to me. He told me that he was a former Dawood aide and was wanted in connection with the killings of music baron Gulshan Kumar, Bollywood actress Manish Koirala's secretary Ajit Dewani, builder Omprakash Kukreja and in more than fifty other cases.

I wondered if our bond existed anymore, since it was based on lies. However, I also knew that Salem had always been nice to me. I'd never seen his other side. I invariably saw him as a kind-hearted person, who helped people. My relationship with him was something very personal and had nothing to do with his association with the mafia. I had never even met anyone else from the mafia—he'd never introduced me to anybody. Also, even after all the lies he had told me, I realised I still loved him. And so, accepting my fate, I decided to give our relationship a chance.

Meanwhile, my parents found out about my affair through the media. Trouble intensified when the media reported that Salem and I had secretly gotten married on 20 November 2000. The news came as a big shock to my family. During the same time, my mother suffered a massive paralytic stroke and was bedridden. I wanted to speak to her but Salem warned me against calling my parents. He told me that the cops would have tapped their phone lines and that I would not only be putting myself at risk but my family as well. So, even as my family repeatedly tried to contact me, I had to keep my distance. I didn't want them to be subjected to any kind of torture because of my foolishness.

In the middle of 2001, we moved to the US as Fauzia

and Danish Beg. According to Salem, the US would be a safe place for us. In fact, after a few weeks, I too began to believe that we were better off now. Salem possessed a non-immigrant work visa in the US, which stated that he was employed as a maintenance manager for a marine engineering company. He and his first wife Samira Jumani had also made a remarkable fortune in the country. Apart from properties worth several crore, they had a two-screen theatre, a gas station and a healthy bank balance. Everything seemed to be getting back to normal for me, when 9/11 happened.

Suddenly, the US seemed like the most unsafe place to be in. A growing feeling of anger and hatred had developed among American citizens, which was evident in the incessant attacks on south Asians and the spate of arrests by the Federal Bureau of Investigation.

Our lives had changed, too. In the weeks following 9/11, Salem became very anxious and insecure. He was never at peace and worried constantly that the FBI would knock at his door one day and take him away. With an Interpol notice slapped against us, Salem's worries only increased. I realised that, behind all his bravado, there was a very timid being. I'd see him spend hours on the phone and the internet, plotting his next step.

When you live with a person for two to three days, he is always good to you. It was when I had been with him for an extended period of time, that I realised we weren't really meant for each other. We were very different.

Our mentalities and our way of thinking were also totally different. When I realised this, I told him that I didn't want to continue living with him. I tried to explain to him that we were very different people but he shut me up every time I brought up the topic.

Then, one day, he told me about his plans to take me on a world tour. He said that he wanted to make up for all the time we had not been able to spend with each other. I could sense something fishy, but I decided to go along with the plan as I too was scared of a possible arrest. Salem's wife Samira—for whom he had set up a home in Texas—was aware of his plans, but was not happy about his decision. Samira had eloped with him when she was barely seventeen and has a son with him. While their relationship had soured over the years and was now beyond repair, I knew that she still cared for him. They both had extensive fights over his plan, until Samira finally allowed him to have his way. I could never forget that she was still legally married to him. I tried to offer her an olive branch but she hated me for obvious reasons.

We finally went on a world tour, visiting a lot of places and meeting many people along the way. These people didn't look at us as criminals on the run but just ordinary people. The trip did a world of good to our relationship. I still remember our six-day trip to Amsterdam. Salem had gone ahead and I followed him after a few days. He met me at the airport with a beautiful bouquet of roses. Later, in the restaurant, he constantly whispered sweet nothings into my ear. He also gifted me a nightgown, after which we made love in our hotel room. Everything was so beautiful. I was surprised by his sudden affection; I didn't know that a man like him could also love so passionately. I could see that Salem was trying his best to woo me back into his life. In the days to come, he became more possessive and respectful towards me. And it wasn't long before I had fallen in love with him once again.

After those memorable days in different parts of the world, we escaped to Lisbon in Portugal. Days became weeks and weeks, months; life had become one endless honeymoon for us. My parents also visited us and were genuinely fond of Salem. My Salem. Everything seemed so wonderful that I had completely forgotten the fact that we had an Interpol notice slapped against us.

Then, on the morning of 20 September 2002, the doorbell rang. We usually didn't have people over, and if we did, we were informed beforehand. Salem told me that it would be better if I checked who our visitor was. Little did I know that I was opening the door to a five-year-long nightmare. A huge phalanx of police officers was standing at my doorstep. They had surrounded our home. Salem tried to resist but we had no option but to surrender.

After our arrest, we were kept in separate cells but were allowed to meet only once a week. The first few days were extremely rough for me. My jail inmates were very disturbing. Unlike me, they were hardcore criminals and aggressive by nature. I hardly interacted with any of them.

I was also worried for Salem. I knew that the arrest would have affected him badly. He'd always been scared of being thrown into the slammer. Fortunately, unlike Indian jails, the Lisbon jail had telephones, so, even though there were restrictions, we kept in touch with each other occasionally. To keep him in good spirits, I also began writing romantic letters to him. I used to refer to him as 'babu', while I would call myself his 'gudiya' (doll). These letters also acted as a way to channel my creativity. I wrote him poems and drew beautiful sketches of us together.

On 20 November 2002, I wrote him a very special letter. It was our second wedding anniversary and we were away from each other. Tears rolled down my cheeks while writing to him. I was saddened by the fact that we weren't in each other's arms that day but instead, in different cells. I wanted him to know how much I loved him and what he meant to me. At this trying stage, I could think of no one but him.

Meanwhile, the Indian government was informed of our arrest and talks of extradition began. My family was also notified and my brother and father hurriedly travelled to Lisbon in the hope of securing my release. However, they soon realised that it would be years before they would see me step out from prison.

In 2003, a Portuguese court, where our case had come up for hearing, sentenced me to two years' imprisonment for entering the country on forged documents. Salem, on the other hand, was sentenced to three years for entering

Portugal on forged documents, two years for causing injury to a cop and resisting his arrest, and one year for perjury.

My father was visibly upset and wouldn't speak to me, until his paternal instincts gave way and he broke down. He looked shattered. I had brought a lot of shame to the family and knew that there was nothing I could do to defend myself. The next two years in Lisbon were emotionally and mentally draining. There wasn't a single day when I was able to sleep peacefully. The years of isolation were taking a toll on me and the battle to survive was eating me from within. The letters to Salem continued even after my family insisted I forget him. Love only acted as a healer and I couldn't explain this to them. However, the continued loneliness had affected me badly and I started seeking a crutch. This was when I found my calling.

The prison authorities had arranged for Christian nuns to visit jail inmates thrice a week to help reform them. I would attend their sessions diligently. It was during this time that a nun, who had noticed me sinking into my own grief, advised me to turn to Christianity. She made me read certain passages in the Bible that actually had a soothing effect on me. I was soon drawn to the teachings of the Bible. I chose not to tell Salem about my inclination towards Christianity. Salem, who is a practising Muslim, had asked me to take up his religion for his sake, and I did not want to hurt his sentiments in any way. My letters to him, though, reduced considerably and we slowly drifted apart. The Bible had given my life a new direction.

In the meantime, something unexpected happened to me in Lisbon. I had given an interview to a TV programme that focused on the lives of jail inmates. I told them my story and how I had been suffering unnecessarily. My interview was aired on a local channel and, before I realised it, I was receiving a lot of support from people. It was during the same time that my brother Bobby told me about the possibility of us being extradited to India in a few months. The nuns had told me that they were praying for me and I felt like God was answering our prayers.

However, Salem, unlike me, did not want to be extradited. He had pleaded with the Portuguese court, stating that he belonged to a minority community in India and that he feared he would be targeted. I, on the other hand, wanted to return. On 10 July 2005, Salem and I had a massive showdown. We had met outside the court after a long time. He was in a bad mood because of my behaviour over the past few months. Apart from not writing letters, I had also begun making excuses to avoid any kind of communication with him. I also refused to greet him with a 'salaam'. He was aware of this sudden change and questioned me about it.

I don't know what got into me, but in a fit of rage I screamed and started fighting with him. I also dragged Samira into our argument and the fact that she was still his wife. Harsh words flew like arrows between us and I came back to my cell crying. It was one of the most agonising days of my life. At night, I wrote to Salem apologising for my behaviour. I told him that I'd had no intention of picking a fight with him and that it had just happened out of the blue.

In the same letter, I decided to tell him about how I could now relate to Christianity. I explained to him why I hadn't been referring to Allah in my letters anymore. I told him that passages of the Bible had captivated me and also asked him to turn towards God for help. I ended the letter on a very devout note saying, 'Babu, God is calling you'. In the deep recesses of my mind, I knew that this would be the last letter I would be writing to him.

From then onwards, the Bible became a permanent fixture in my hand. I prayed night and day, asking for forgiveness and help. My prayers were finally answered. In the first week of November 2005, I was told to pack my bags for India. After a lot of legal wrangling, the Indian government had assured Portuguese authorities that Salem and I wouldn't be given death sentences or life terms if convicted. I thanked God profusely. I was now going back where I belonged.

Chapter 4

SCURRYING FOR THE SMALL SCREEN

After a half-hour's grilling, the Intelligence Bureau handed Salem over to the CBI. This was the first of the several sessions the IB would have with him. Once, with the CBI, Salem kept on pleading with officials to allow him to meet Monica privately one last time. By then, women officials from the Hyderabad CBI had also arrived. Pardesi decided to grant Salem his final request but denied him a private tête-à-tête.

And so, before Monica was taken to Hyderabad, Salem got his last opportunity to see her. Pardesi observed that while Salem tried to have a word with her, Monica showed no interest and didn't say much except for goodbye. Then, Salem knew that she was done with him for good.

Monica was flown to Hyderabad on an Indian Airlines flight. She spent her night at the CBI office in the Koti area of Hyderabad. The following day she was taken to court, where she was remanded to judicial custody for seeking a passport under a fictitious name from the Kurnool district of Andhra Pradesh.

When she landed in India, Monica had assumed her ordeal was almost over. She did not realise that she would be taken into custody by the Indian authorities and that the judgment would lead to another extended stay behind bars for her.

For the next ten months, she was lodged at the Chanchalguda Jail in Hyderabad, with her bail pleas repeatedly being rejected by the court. Initially, even her lawyer and relatives weren't allowed to meet her. In September 2006, Monica was sentenced to five years' rigorous imprisonment by the special court of the CBI in Hyderabad on the charges of cheating, criminal conspiracy and impersonation while securing a fake passport. Two months later, on 25 November, she was shifted to the Central Jail in Bhopal for allegedly securing another fake passport from there. All this while, Monica didn't protest.

It was seventeen months after her extradition from Portugal before she finally broke her silence. She wrote a letter to the court from Central Jail stating that she was innocent. 'I was very young and inexperienced and a plain and simple girl by nature. I was without a guardian in Mumbai and desired to develop my future as an artiste. I was ignorant about many evils that were prevalent in Mumbai. I couldn't imagine the pros and cons. I never thought that for such innocence and ignorance, I would be subjected to so much suffering in India,' she wrote.

Two months later, on 16 July 2007, the Bhopal court absolved her of all charges in the fake passport case. But Monica was only able to walk free when the special CBI court in Hyderabad granted her bail on 24 July 2007. After her release, Monica spoke at length to the media about her experience in Indian jails. 'For the first time, I came face to face with real poverty and injustice. There were many women languishing behind bars for crimes they had never committed, while there were others who openly boasted of their criminal exploits yet managed to be set free. But my jail inmates loved me. They would cook for me, do other chores for me. I, on the other hand, would teach them to dance and give them some beauty tips. The girls were so thrilled that someone they saw on the screen was amongst them,' Monica said.

Salem's deepest fears came true when the starlet openly claimed that she no longer pined for him. 'I loved him but all his actions were selfish. He duped me. There cannot be another chapter between Salem and me,' she said. It was clear that Monica wanted to forget her past and start afresh. Her only advantage was that Salem was still languishing in Arthur Road Jail.

But Bollywood's very own controversy's child didn't seem to have seen the end of it. Exactly a month after she was released, TV channels and newspapers carried purported nude pictures of Monica, which were allegedly shot with hidden cameras from inside Central Jail. The pictures 'horrified and pained' the actress, she said; her right to life and dignity had been violated. India's apex court immediately passed a judgement in her favour and restrained the media from showing the nude pictures.

Meanwhile, Monica rented a modest flat at Mulund in suburban Mumbai and began picking up the pieces of her life. She was determined to gain all that she had lost in Mumbai. During this time, she also gave a lot of interviews to the media to garner public sympathy and increase her support base. A year had passed since the ordeal but Monica was still living a life of obscurity. Then in 2008, *Bigg Boss 2* happened. The reality show—along the lines of UK's *Big Brother*—was launched in India, several months before Bollywood actress Shilpa Shetty won the *Celebrity Big Brother* title in UK in 2007. When the producers offered Monica a chance to be part of the second season of the show in August 2008, she grabbed the opportunity.

Within a few episodes, Monica managed to woo the other fourteen contestants and the audience. In one of the episodes, she broke down and said she needed the prize money because she was leading a hand-to-mouth existence. 'The prize is very important. It holds a lot of meaning for me. People think Monica Bedi has a lot of money. But it is not true. I need this money to buy a home. Nobody gives me a house on rent because people are scared of me. I am here to change the image that the media has created of me. I want them to know the real Monica. I am not as bad as people think I am. I want to do it more for my parents than for myself. I have put them through a lot of shame,' she said, between sobs.

Monica's performance on national television won the heart of millions, including Congress Member of Parliament Sanjay Nirupam, who was one of the participants on the show. In fact, Nirupam promised to give her an apartment in the upmarket residential colony of Lokhandwala in Andheri. Monica was evicted from the show within a few weeks, only to return as a wild card entrant.

What followed was more controversial fodder for the media. Stories of Monica becoming romantically involved with another notorious participant and political heir Rahul Mahajan started doing the rounds. Rahul, a self-proclaimed Casanova, was constantly seen wooing and flirting with her during the show. He indirectly proposed marriage to her and asked if he could kiss her. Monica was also seen pouring her heart out to him. All their antics were caught on camera.

Salem, still behind bars, slapped her with a legal notice. It read, 'You (Monica) are a married woman and if you want to marry some other man, you will first have to obtain a divorce from me (Salem).'

When Monica was evicted from the show again in November, she publicly claimed that Rahul was a 'very close friend' and that she needed some time before she could commit to him. However, as soon as Rahul came out of the show, he cleared the air and denied that he would be marrying her. 'I am not marrying her. She is a dear friend and I will always stand by her. I only want people to treat her with respect,' he explained. A visibly upset Monica surprisingly maintained a cold silence. Weeks later she told the media that Rahul was 'not her kind of guy'.

There is no doubting that *Bigg Boss* changed Monica Bedi's life to a certain extent. While she is still not able to find a footing in Bollywood, Indian television has opened its arms to her. Monica has since been seen in several television shows after this, including the dance show *Jhalak Dhikhla Ja*.

In 2009 she launched a religious music album, *Ek Omkara*, where she chants verses from the Guru Granth Sahib. A Sikh by birth, Monica had taken to Islam and Christianity, before turning back to Sikhism. Her only defence for shifting religious loyalties was that she was very spiritually inclined. 'I can't sing but chanting from the sacred texts of my religious book has helped me get in touch with my spiritual side,' she said.

For a woman with dreams of making it big in the Hindi film industry, it is ironic that Monica's own life reads like the screenplay of a Bollywood masala film. She has seen the good, the bad and the ugly, and yet her dreams still seem far from being realised.

EPILOGUE

'I am extremely sorry for the delay,' she said, as she sat down opposite us, her publicist joining her on the couch. 'This show is so competitive ... I have been practising with my choreographer all day, so I just got caught up. Sorry again,' she added.

Monica was dressed in a green T-shirt and blue jeans that showed off her slim figure. Her wavy hair, with golden-brown streaks on it, was let loose and she barely had any make-up on her face, except for gloss on her lips. A few people threw knowing glances at her but Monica seemed indifferent as she made herself comfortable on the small cane couch.

The meeting had been fixed after a lot of unanswered calls and ignored messages. She had finally agreed to meet us over coffee at the JW Marriott Hotel in suburban Mumbai, following repeated requests to her publicist Shradha. Monica was late by over forty-five minutes, but was apologetic, very unlike a celebrity. The show she was referring to was the third season of *Jhalak Dikhla Ja,* which was going to hit Indian television in the second week of April 2009. Monica seemed very nervous about the dance show. 'Cut-throat competition,' she said succinctly.

The sole purpose of the meeting was to convince her to talk to us for the book. 'I am not so sure about this. The past few months have been so good and I have been so lucky that I don't want to rake up my past anymore,' she said.

'But don't you want to clear the air?'

'I don't feel the need to. People have started accepting me despite my past. You've seen it on *Bigg Boss*,' she said, sipping her black coffee. We noticed that she was deliberately avoiding the topic of Salem in our conversation.

Despite her reluctance, we explained the premise of our book to her. Monica listened carefully and, for a moment, she seemed intrigued. 'Even if we do the project, how would I have to contribute?' she asked.

'Just a few sittings with us, where you can tell us your real story.'

'Hmm … you know, many people have offered to do a film on my life but I've refused.'

'Why?'

'I want to forget my past. It was traumatic,' she said.

'But your story is very interesting …'

'Yes, I know. Interesting for others, not for me, which is why I have got the copyright of my story,' she said.

'How can you have a copyright to your story, when it is out in the media and heavily recorded in police dossiers?'

She didn't reply for a few seconds. Then she said, 'Uh ... I will have to speak to my parents before I get back to you on this. They take all my decisions for me.'

We agreed, and then asked her about other issues including her comeback on reality television shows, her alleged relationship with Rahul Mahajan and her recent decision to launch a religious music album. Though uncomfortable, she answered all our questions cautiously. When she had sipped the last of her coffee, she got up to leave. We shook hands, even as she promised to get back to us in two days.

The call never came, neither were any of our calls to her received.

SIX

WIVES OF HINDU DONS

INTRODUCTION

That the female of the species is deadlier than the male.

—*Rudyard Kipling*

The implication of these lines from Kipling's century- old poem still remains a subject of contention and debate. Nevertheless, in Mumbai's mafia history, this rings true, as exemplified by the wives of dons, who emerged as powerful de facto bosses following unexpected developments in the city's crime scene.

In the mid 1990s, with the surge of terrorism, both the state and international police began closing in on the underworld, sounding the death knell for Mumbai's mafiosi. Or so the police thought. In order to avoid direct confrontation with the law and to deflect the attention of the police, mafia bosses handed the reins of their respective 'businesses' over to the people they trusted the most.

However, with cases of defection on the rise and the ganglords' lack of faith in their own men, finding a custodian became a challenge. Time was short and options were decreasing by the minute. In this environment of distrust, many dons turned to their better halves. Until then, these significant others had looked on from the sidelines as their husbands carried out their bloody work. Their lives were restricted to carrying out households chores and chanting bhajans in makeshift temples in their homes. Suddenly, these very same wives found themselves in a situation that required them to expand their management skills, from their homes to an entire gang.

Dealing with a pack of hoodlums, they soon realised, wasn't as easy as rearing a family. Yet, like the perfect Bharatiya naari, who swears to protect her husband from the enemy, these women took their place in the world of organised crime. With chutzpah, they shed their timid and cocooned selves to turn into conniving, ambitious, competitive and sharp women. Soon, their involvement became so vital to the gang that the dons could not imagine isolating their wives from any of their activities.

These housewives now ordered executions, threatened people and ran huge crime syndicates. While Padma, the ambitious wife of former Rajan aide Ravi Poojary, chose to stay on the sidelines and work as the brain of her husband's gang, other wives dabbled in politics, social activism and white-collar jobs to keep their husbands' gangs in the big business of bloodshed, with a regular flow of income. For instance, Sujata Nikhalje, wife of fugitive don Chhota Rajan, started a million-dollar real estate enterprise to legitimise her husband's criminal activities. Asha Gawli, a devotional singer and the wife of underworld don-turned-politician Arun Gawli, helped her husband start his own political party, and used it to protect him against fake encounters. Ashwin Naik's wife Neeta, on the other hand, persuaded her London-educated engineer husband to join the crime syndicate. Ashwin eventually became a hardened gangster while Neeta took to politics, to shield his activities.

As a result of this passing of the baton, the police, who until then seemed determined to nip the underworld in the bud, suddenly began to falter. This unexpected power shift, at least for a while, threw their investigations out of gear.

These women rattled the police as they climbed the criminal ladder to become 'Mummy' and 'Nani' to petty criminals and hardened gangsters alike. These are the stories of Asha Gawli, Neeta Naik, Sujata Nikhalje and Padma Poojary.

ASHA GAWLI

An elderly gentleman strolls up to a small but predominantly Muslim crowd of old and middle-aged men gathered outside a slum in Mumbai's Byculla area. The gentleman is tall and big-built, yet unimposing. His right hand spends a large part of its time caressing his flowing white beard as he takes his place with the crowd that is evidently waiting for someone. The men, speaking in hushed tones, pause to warmly greet the seventy-something-year-old gentleman and call passers-by over to be part of their gathering.

When the car they've been waiting for finally pulls up in front of the slum, the men draw closer, led by the man with the flowing white beard. They raise their right fists to yell in unison, 'Mummy zindabad! Mummy zindabad!'

'Mummy', clad in a green saree, steps out and smiles in appreciation of their overwhelming reception. To an outsider, the admiration and adoration she is receiving from this elderly crowd of Muslim men, who address her as 'mother', would appear strange—with her jet-black hair and only-slightly lined brown skin, she doesn't appear to be a day over fifty. It's not by virtue of her age or that she was born a Muslim, that she enjoys this respect and adulation; it is the fact that she is married to the Hindu don, Arun Gawli, christened 'Daddy' by the locals of the area.

Today, she is here to campaign for Daddy, the candidate of an otherwise insignificant party in the state's political circuit. The gathering listens with rapt attention as she asks them, with her hands folded humbly, to vote for her husband to get a second-term in the state assembly.

With her symbolic vermillion and mangalsutra, Asha Gawli portrays convincingly the humble Hindu wife, someone to be pitied because her 'social worker husband', wrongly framed by the cops, is currently behind bars. Police records, however, sketch a very different picture of Asha Gawli.

Asha can be credited with safeguarding her husband against the police machinery, and fake encounters on innumerable occasions. She helped her husband float his own political party, the Akhil Bharatiya Sena. Due to her efforts, Arun eventually went on to become a member of the Legislative Assembly in the state government. With a strong ally in his wife, it is not surprising that Arun is practically the only don who has been able to stay on in Mumbai and shape a career in crime and politics, right under the nose of the police and the Maharashtra government.

Arun was already an established gangster when he married Zubeida Mujawar, aka Asha. Like his father, he had first landed himself a job at Shakti Mills in Mahalaxmi at the young age of twenty. It was when Arun shifted to Crompton Greaves Ltd in Kanjurmarg, that he began to get involved with the underworld. He joined hands with his old friend and schoolmate Rama Naik, and the two got involved in several local intra-gang brawls. He shot to fame when he, along with his accomplice Naik and another goon Babu Reshim (a leader of the canteen workers in the Mazgaon docks), murdered Parasnath Pandey—who ran major matka and liquor rackets—in 1980. They killed Pandey in order to gain control of the collection of matka and liquor money in central Mumbai.

Arun was consequently detained under the National Security Act but was released after a month of custody. His power and influence grew after his release from jail. It is during this time that he met and fell in love with seventeen-year-old Zubeida who, like Arun, lived in Byculla. Zubeida's marriage had already been arranged with a boy from within the Muslim community, but when Arun asked her to marry him, she accepted happily. Naik and Reshim opposed the alliance on the grounds that the two were from different communities; they were aghast that Arun, a Hindu Maharashtrian, was marrying a Muslim. Arun refused to budge, and finally married Zubedia, who then converted to Hinduism and changed her name to Asha. In her, Arun came to find a dependable aide and a woman who would run his household at Dagdi Chawl in Byculla.

Asha, who went on to give birth to five children (Geeta, Mahesh, Yogita, Yogesh and Asmita), initially stayed away from her husband's criminal activities. She raised and educated her children and watched anxiously from a distance as Arun indulged in the bloody battles of the mafiosi.

However, with Arun being a frequent guest in jails in the city, Asha had no option but to take the reins and run the show by proxy. This she did, very effectively, and went on to formulate ingenious ways to protect her husband from the law. Holes were dug inside their kitchen in which Arun would hide whenever the police arrived with an arrest warrant. According to the police, Asha had a pit dug right below the area that housed the gas cylinder.

Soon her involvement became so vital to the gang that Arun began treating her as his most trusted lieutenant. Over the years, Asha's demeanour changed, as she shed her shy and orthodox ways and turned aggressive and wily in her dealings. Since Arun's gang members addressed him as 'Daddy', Asha automatically came to be known as 'Mummy'.

In 1996, when Arun was locked up in the Kolhapur jail and serving time under the Terrorist and Disruptive Activities Act (TADA), I paid him a visit for a story. At the time, he had fleetingly mentioned his aspirations to join politics. The reason—to save himself from a police encounter. The previous year, Asha had stood for the civic corporation elections, hoping her political standing would help her husband but she had lost terribly. After this, she shifted her focus to her husband's political career. In 1997, with his wife's encouragement and support, he started the Akhil Bharatiya Sena. While he was the president of the ABS, Asha headed the women's wing. It is the women's wing which was used as a shield for the don against arrests and police encounters. A group of women would constantly surround Arun every time he walked out of Dagdi Chawl—something that other dons in the underworld made fun of. But the strategy worked. The cops could neither trace him in the crowd nor get violent with the women, hence he was able to escape unscathed on more than one occasion.

In 1998, Asha herself was arrested for her involvement in the Manish Shah murder case.

Shah, a partner of industrialist Vallabh Thakkar, was killed on 2 February 1998 near his Sagar Mahal residence at Malabar Hill. Police investigations revealed that Shah had been shot by four of Arun's henchmen, at his command. At the time of the murder, the ABS president had been detained at the Amravati Central Prison, under the Maharashtra Prevention of Dangerous Activities Act.

Later, the police stumbled upon some tiny slips of paper during a raid of Arun's home in Dagdi Chawl. One of these contained a note concerning Manish Shah. It read, '*Asha, Rajala saangun Bandyakadun Manish Shahache kam laukar karun ghe.*' (Asha, tell Raja to get Bandya to deal with the Manish Shah matter immediately.)

Express Newsline carried a series of stories and reports that exposed Asha's covert involvement in her husband's mafia activities. Under interrogation, Arun confessed to sending the chit addressed to his wife while he was in prison in January 1998. Asha was later released on bail, for lack of evidence, but the police now started keeping close watch on her.

Subsequently, Asha, in an interview to a tabloid, said she knew that Arun was a criminal but supported him primarily because she loved him. She also said that she longed for a normal life but knew that it could never happen. 'But I love Arun more than I love myself. Without him, I am nothing. I will do anything for him,' she said.

In 2002, the ABS contested the Brihanmumbai Municipal Corporation elections. In its very first attempt at entering the city's civic body, two corporators were elected—Arun's eldest daughter Geeta Gawli and Sunil

Ghate, who was a one-time contract killer. In 2004, Asha's management and supervision of Arun's political party finally bore fruit when her husband was elected the MLA from the Byculla constituency. In the same year, Asha was once again arrested, this time for assaulting a woman. Asha, along with her two of her domestic helpers, Archana Kate and Bhavana Patil, was arrested on 20 December 2004 for assaulting a woman called Sushma Sawant with sticks. The trio was released on the same day, after they were granted bail on a surety of Rs 3,000 each. Incidentally, Asha had filed a complaint about the theft of her daughter's ornaments, and had accused Sushma's son. Asha had called Sushma home to enquire about her son but the meeting had resulted in a verbal duel between the two, after which Asha and her domestic help had beaten Sushma.

With her husband's encouragement, Asha launched a music company and churned out several albums of paeans to her deity. Despite the songs having no takers, her company Aai Music Service seemed to rake in big profits. When the Income Tax department announced amnesty under the Voluntary Disclosure of Income Scheme (VDIS) a couple of years ago, the don admitted to an annual income of over Rs 1 crore. By 2004, when Arun filed the statutory income statement before fighting the state elections, the income of his music company had swelled to Rs 2 crore.

A couple of years before the Legislative Assembly elections of 2009, Gawli was again put behind bars. This time he was being tried under the Maharashtra Control of

Organised Crime Act (MCOCA).* However, Asha didn't give up. She filed his nomination papers for him, and along with her daughter Geeta, took it upon herself to campaign for him. A pre-election report in *The Asian Age* by Jigna Vora also mentioned how Agni, an NGO, had rated Arun the most competent MLA during his term. In fact, it had been Asha who had worked in the constituency on her husband's behalf. While Arun spent most of his time as an MLA in jail, Asha had ensured that she redressed the grievances of the people in the locality, as she knew that only their satisfaction could give her husband another shot at the MLA seat. While campaigning, she spent money from the gang's resources to ensure that people were happy with her husband. However, they did not stop to think about one crucial aspect—Arun's own absence. Besides, his lack of attendance in the Assembly session hadn't gone unnoticed by political observers. The people of his constituency voted against him and Arun failed to clinch the MLA post.

Mummy, however, is not a disappointed woman. For her, the very fact that Arun is safe and unharmed by police forces, even after being tried under several stringent laws, still makes her a clear winner. Several top dons

* MCOCA is a stringent law promulgated by the Maharashtra government in 1998 after the abrogation of the TADA. Since they did not have any firm law with which to fight organised crime, the state government formulated this law. Later, the Gujarat and Delhi governments used the same law to control criminal gangs.

like Amar Naik, Sada Pawle and Nari Khan have been killed in fake police encounters. In fact, even low-level acolytes have not been spared by the cops. If Gawli has managed to survive the encounters, and even gone on to win MLA elections, and if his daughter and party workers have become corporators, it's largely because of his wife. Arun Gawli rarely steps out of his fortress; it is Asha who goes out and does everything for him, whether it's canvassing for elections, making the rounds of the courts for legal battles or staging dharnas outside police stations and ministers' offices.

And as long as Asha has the support of the hordes who thronged her Byculla rally on the campaign trail, Mummy and Daddy's days of working outside and around the system are far from numbered.

NEETA NAIK

'I breathe Ashwin. I don't need food or water to survive; only my fond memories of him,' Neeta Naik, wife of fugitive gangster Ashwin Naik, told me in an interview from the comforts of her gaudily furnished tenement No. 144 at Subashnagar in Byculla in 1997. A powerful statement coming from a strong-willed politician and commanding civic corporator.

I remembered this statement, and her large sunken eyes and the impossibly high cheekbones that reminded me of Hollywood actor Maggie Gyllenhal, three years later, when I awoke to the news that Neeta had been murdered by her husband.

Ashwin, who apparently suspected his wife of infidelity, allegedly had her killed by his henchmen. It was a gruesome end to the fairytale romance of a couple who had both loved and lived dangerously.

Neeta and Ashwin Naik's story dates back to the early 1980s. She was a convent-schooled Gujarati girl from the upmarket south Mumbai locale of Breach Candy, while he was Maharashtrian and the brother of the vegetable vendor- turned-don Amar Naik. The couple was very much in love but their relationship suffered when news of it reached the ears of Neeta's family.

Neeta went on to complete her Bachelor of Arts from Sophia College while Ashwin moved to London to study for a degree in electrical engineering. Despite the distance, their affair continued.

On Ashwin's return from London, the couple eloped and got married despite severe opposition from Neeta's orthodox Gujarati family. The first few years of marriage were happy ones; soon, however, Ashwin—upset with the stigma of being the brother of a don—decided to move to Chennai with his family. He and Neeta made a couple of trips to Chennai to find a house. It was on their return from one of these trips, in 1991, that the couple had an encounter with death. It was an incident that would change their life completely.

On his way back home from the Santa Cruz airport

in Mumbai, Ashwin's car was attacked by members of the Chhota Rajan gang. Neeta and her father-in-law were in another car behind his. Panic and chaos hit the Kherwadi highway as around twenty men opened fire at Ashwin's car. Knowing that her husband was unarmed, Neeta stopped her own car, got out, and began screaming, hoping that someone would call the police. By then, Ashwin had dodged the bullets and managed to make an unlikely escape. 'It was then that I knew my husband was unsafe. I told Ashwin that I wanted him alive and not dead. For this, I didn't mind if he had to join hands with his own brother and become part of the crime syndicate,' Neeta revealed in her 1997 interview.

After much persuasion from his wife, Ashwin finally gave in and joined the underworld. He went on to become the first educationally-qualified gangster in Mumbai's mafia circuit.

Over time, Ashwin became known for his meticulous planning and organisational abilities. People still remember him for the killing of Tanya Koli in a Kalyan local train and the murder of textile tycoon Sunit Khatau in Mahalaxmi. Ashwin was later arrested under TADA but this did not deter him. After Chhota Rajan's split from Dawood, Ashwin became an ally of the latter and was thus able to build a strong criminal base for himself. All along, Neeta remained his pillar of support; she was his close confidante and personal advisor.

The first cracks in their marriage developed early in

1992, when, much against her husband's wishes, Neeta decided to join Bal Thackeray's Shiv Sena and stand for municipal elections.

Though Neeta considered politics a 'dirty business', she wanted to carve out an identity of her own; she was also aware of the possibility of her political clout being used to legitimise her husband's activities. It came as no surprise when she won the elections by a huge majority. Later, she attributed the win to her husband, as she knew that people voted for her because they feared her husband. But she was determined to be an efficient corporator and earn herself a good name. She now began to live a double life—as a politician and as a gangster's wife.

Meanwhile, Ashwin's powerful affiliations began to hurt Dawood's rival Arun Gawli. In 1994, Gawli's men shot at Ashwin and rendered him wheelchair-bound for life. With rival gangs and the police closing in on him, Ashwin took a flight to safety and fled to Canada, then South Africa and Singapore, leaving his wife and two children in Mumbai. After his escape, the couple did not keep in touch—a deliberate move on Neeta's part. She knew her phone lines were being tapped and whereabouts closely monitored and she did not want to do anything to jeopardise her political career. Although she knew all Ashwin's gang members by their first names, she had never personally involved herself in any of their extortion activities. Now she distanced herself even more from them.

The police never really maintained any dossier on her,

because she was not a criminal. The special branch only had a thin file on Neeta, which stated that she had been in touch with her husband while he was absconding and that she had handled his finances for a while. Neeta, however, feigned innocence and portrayed herself as the wife of a misguided man, forced to fight her own battles.

Now, with Ashwin on the run, Neeta began enjoying her new-found freedom. She was making her presence felt in the Shiv Sena, despite the party not being entirely open to recruiting women. Her convent education had proved an advantage in her dealings with people; further, she was also making an impact as a powerful orator in the standing committee meetings of the Bombay Municipal Corporation, as it was then called. It is this political acumen and connections that won Neeta acceptance among the masses and another term in the BMC in 1995. While her sister- in-law Anjali Naik (wife of Amar Naik) and Asha Gawli (wife of Arun Gawli) had also contested for the 1995 municipal elections, it was only Neeta who managed to secure a berth in the BMC.

With her husband still absconding, Neeta made it clear that the victory was her own and no one else's. She was educated, shrewd and a quick learner, making her a valuable member of the Shiv Sena. Now, with a second term in hand, she also had easy access to Sena chief Bal Thackeray at his Matoshree residence in Bandra. This period of self- realisation created another wide crack in the Neeta-Ashwin relationship. By then, the separation period had been a few years and Neeta was beginning to feel very lonely. Both Ashwin and Neeta had tried their best to shield their two children from the shadows of the world of crime and provide them with a good education. But the lonely battle was getting to her and she began to look for support elsewhere. And she allegedly found it in private bodyguard Laxmi Zhiman.

In August 1999, the police arrested Ashwin while he was trying to cross the border from Bangladesh into India. He was sent to Tihar jail. A week later, Neeta in an interview to a tabloid, said that his homecoming was not really a celebration. 'I am back to being Ashwin Naik's wife. I can't face people. I just can't fight anymore ... no, I don't regret being Ashwin Naik's wife but I do regret my whole existence ... I want to meet him and talk about our future together.'

The media had written a lot about Neeta's alleged extramarital affair. Ashwin apparently could not stomach her relations with Zhiman. Always a possessive man, he had earlier ordered the killing of electrical contractor Eknath Khanvilkar after he worked in his house for a few weeks and had supposedly been intimate with Neeta Naik. The final straw for him was when he, through his henchmen, acquired photographs that had captured Zhiman and Neeta together.

On 13 November 2000, Neeta arrived at her Byculla home around noon. As she got to the door and was unlocking it, two men—identified as Manoj Bhalekar and Sunil Jadhav—brutally gunned her down. Neeta was rushed to KEM Hospital in Parel where she succumbed to her injuries a day later.

The following day, the media was filled with stories of Neeta's murder. Her liaisons with other men were ascribed as the cause for her tragic end. Unfortunately, this end was said to have come at the hands of her own husband, the very person she had encouraged into the world of crime.

After Neeta's murder, five persons were arrested but two of them were later acquitted. Three others—Bhalekar, Nilratan Mukherjee and Jadhav—were convicted. Jadhav was later killed in an encounter. Based on the confessions of Bhalekar and Mukherjee, Ashwin, who was already behind bars, was charged under the special MCOCA for the murder of his wife. According to police records, the conspiracy was hatched by the gangster while inside Tihar jail.

On 31 January 2009, a special MCOCA court acquitted Ashwin of his wife's murder for lack of evidence and the Ashwin-Neeta love story that had turned sour, was finally shut for good.

SUJATA NIKHALJE

A decade ago, Tilak Nagar was an obscure lower-middle class residential locality in suburban Mumbai, dotted with decrepit government quarters. One woman with ambitious designs wanted to change the whole topography of this area and transform it into upmarket real estate for the crème de la crème of the city. This woman was Sujata Nikhalje, alias Nani, wife of self-proclaimed patriotic don Rajendra Sadashiv Nikhalje, alias Chhota Rajan. Sujata Nikhalje is also the only 'don wife' to have been slapped with charges under the MCOCA for using a business enterprise to legitimise her husband's criminal activities.

Early in the year 2000, Sujata Nikhalje started a construction company with the ill-gotten money of her fugitive husband, despite having no knowledge of the industry. Surprisingly, her company soon began leading the race in remodelling Tilak Nagar into an upmarket suburban destination in Mumbai. It was only a little while before the police learned that Sujata, through her business, was playing financial manager and banker to Rajan.

With agencies such as the Directorate of Revenue Intelligence, Mumbai police's Crime Branch, Enforcement Directorate and the Income Tax department of India keeping tabs on her activities, Sujata earned herself a very menacing reputation.

Sujata and Rajan lived in the same neighbourhood when they fell in love. She lived in a government chawl in Tilak Nagar and Rajan, a native of Lonar village in Satara, lived near Sahakar Cinema in the same area. Rajan dropped out of school after Class 5 and went on to join a group of boys who used to tout film tickets on the black market in front of Sahakar Cinema.

Rajan first came into the limelight in 1979 when he

took the lead in assaulting police officers of the Tilak Nagar police station who were trying to stop the black marketing of movie tickets. He then joined local gangster Rajan Nair, alias Bada (big) Rajan. Following Nair's murder, Rajan decided to step into his mentor's shoes and take over the reins of the gang, which is how he eventually earned the title of Chhota (small) Rajan. Later, he affiliated himself with underworld don Dawood Ibrahim, at whose behest he began handling all the activities of the D-gang in Mumbai.

It was somewhere around this time that Rajan and Sujata fell in love. He was a notorious goon, feared amongst the people of the Tilak Nagar area, while she was a girl from a simple lower middle-class Maharashtrian family. Rajan's growing reputation in Tilak Nagar as a prominent gangster only drew Sujata closer to him. They both eventually fell in love. Rajan and Sujata's courting period came to a brief standstill when the former, fearing arrests by the Mumbai police, escaped the city and moved to Dubai to be with his boss, Dawood. Fortunately for their romance, the separation period was brief.

In 1987, within a year of his escape, Rajan called Sujata to Dubai and the couple was married in a special ceremony arranged by Dawood. A photograph taken at the wedding—showing Dawood and his wife Mehjebeen standing beside the newlyweds Rajan and Sujata—was splashed across the Indian media. Dawood and Rajan were very close at this time, so much so that years later, their relationship was depicted on celluloid by Bollywood director Ram Gopal Verma in his film *Company*.

In 1993, Rajan split from the D-company and went into hiding somewhere in Southeast Asia. Meanwhile, Sujata flew back home to India with her three young daughters Ankita, Nikita and Khushi. Rajan went on to build a huge business empire, which included extortion, property deals, the film industry, gambling and betting dens, prostitution rackets and horse racing. For some time, his trusted associates looked after his properties across India. However, Rajan lost some of his close aides to police encounters and bullets from the enemy camp, including his most capable hitman and financier Rohit Verma, who was killed by the henchmen of Dawood aide Chhota Shakeel. Over the next couple of years, Rajan was left with no trustworthy second- in-command. With a mini-empire in Mumbai itself, Rajan needed someone to handle both his finances and extortion business in the city. But a series of betrayals had made him wary of his own men. So Rajan looked homewards for support to prop up his financial empire, and found the desired handler in his wife. A housewife and mother of three daughters, Sujata was suddenly pushed into taking up the reins of her husband's illegitimate empire.

Sujata began to slowly and steadily expand Rajan's extortion business and supervise the activities of his gang from the comfort of her home in Tilak Nagar. She soon went on to be recognised as Nani, a sobriquet she earned not because she was grandmother to anyone but because she was the wife of Rajan, alias Nana.

According to the police, because of her lack of knowledge in business and finances, Sujata initially worked with a group of consultants to get a clearer picture of her husband's financial stocks and to seek advice on how her husband's businesses could be legitimised. Her advisors zeroed in on Bollywood and the real estate industry, as they were businesses where black money could be invested. However, Sujata's brother-in-law, Deepak Nikhalje, had recently been hit by allegations of using his brother's money to fund a film. In 1999, he had produced the Hindi film *Vaastav,* starring actor Sanjay Dutt. When *Vaastav* became a hit, the media raised a hue and cry as they thought that Deepak was a front for his gangster brother. Deepak had a hard time proving that it was his own money and not his brother's that had funded the film. This storm deterred Sujata from investing in films because, if the brother could be accused of being a front, then the wife would be a surefire target of such allegations. So Sujata went for the other option—real estate.

In the late '90s, real estate and rental prices were soaring across Mumbai and builders were looking for better prospects beyond the city. Tilak Nagar, which until then had been merely a 'township colony' comprising wide open spaces and old buildings, was an attractive destination for redevelopment. Builders had already started taking an interest in the area and had begun redeveloping old buildings. More often than not, Sujata's intervention was required. With her reputation as 'Nani' and wife of a gangster, Sujata often managed to arm-twist several people into selling their homes for good prices.

Soon, realising the money-spinning options in the construction business, Sujata began her own construction company, Khushi Developers Private Ltd, named after her youngest daughter. But before she went into business, she employed a powerful team of chartered accountants to handle the finances of the company. With their help, she prepared a strategy to slowly transform Tilak Nagar into a plush suburban locality, pulling down old buildings and replacing them with sprawling malls, high-rises and office complexes. Sujata turned into a corporate don wife, meeting builders through the day and signing deals worth crores of rupees.

Throughout, she kept Rajan informed of these meetings via telephone calls. Following the advice of her husband, she also involved his men to ensure she had her way. Often, Rajan's goons would terrorise builders through extortion and land-grabbing. Due to the fear psychosis generated among the builders and the common masses by Rajan's gang, Sujata managed to run her business smoothly. This honeymoon period, however, didn't last long.

The police, who had been tapping Sujata's phone lines, learned that, while speaking to Rajan, her conversations would often drift into the acquisition of land and deals. Sensing that something was up, the police decided to close in on her. At the same time, one of the builders from a society in Chembur who had been threatened by Rajan's gang in a building contract deal, filed a complaint with the police. This witness provided the police with the much-needed impetus for their case.

Following the complaint and police inquiries, Sujata and three other accomplices, i.e., Suresh Shyamrao Shinde alias Don, Harvinder Singh Bedi alias Kukku Daruwala and Rakesh Surver, were arrested under the MCOCA on 14 December 2005, on charges of aiding and abetting the activities of an organised crime syndicate run by Chhota Rajan. Though Sujata was remanded to police custody till 27 December 2005, the police initially found it very difficult to make any headway in the case. Allegedly, by this time Sujata had become so hardened and obstinate, that she refused to drink water or eat anything during the first sixteen days of custody.

Police investigations showed that Sujata maintained thirty-seven accounts in various banks, including Standard Chartered, State Bank of India, Sangli Bank, Canara Bank and the Union Bank of India. These bank accounts were in the names of her three daughters. The police suspected that the money in these accounts came from extortion payments from India and abroad but were passed off as goodwill donations in the name of the three daughters. Foreign exchange worth Rs 13 lakh had also come into these accounts from countries like Singapore and Abu Dhabi. Sujata maintained that these were voluntary contributions made by businessmen and well-wishers, a claim that the police was not willing to accept. Following this, all her accounts were frozen.

For the police, the manner in which the money had been safely stacked in banks across the country pointed towards external help. Further investigations revealed the involvement of a prominent chartered accountant, identified as Bharat Dhudani who allegedly handled the financial transactions of the real estate projects of Khushi Developers. The police alleged that Sujata had given Rs 2 crore (obtained from Rajan) to Dhudani, who gave it to eight firms to buy shares in her company. The police traced most of Sujata's accounts through documents, which included fourteen files found at Dhudani's Bandra office.

At one stage, the police realised that the whole case was getting very complicated. Hence, the police sought the help of the Directorate of Revenue Intelligence, Mumbai police's Crime Branch, Enforcement Directorate and the Income Tax department of India to help them put the pieces together. With their help, the police managed to get enough evidence to incriminate her and Sujata was charge-sheeted under the MCOCA in 2006.

After spending two years in jail, Sujata was finally released on a bail bond of Rs 1 lakh on 12 September 2007, as the police failed to prove the charges against her. Since then, the police has been working towards presenting a watertight case against her; she, on her part, has roped in a battery of professional lawyers to defend her.

In 2008, Sujata requested permission from the court to travel to Hong Kong and Singapore to help get her daughter Anita admitted to a foreign university, and also to defreeze her bank account to fund her daughter's education. Both her demands were opposed by the Enforcement Directorate as they saw it as an attempt by her to flee the country and stay with Rajan. The ED stated that the investigation against Sujata under the Money Laundering Act was in its final stage, hence her application was rejected.

For now Sujata is lying low in order to avoid any further confrontation with the law. However, she continues to enjoy the privilege of being Tilak Nagar's Nani. And as long as she can do so, neither she nor her husband has much to worry about.

PADMA POOJARY

Question: What does an educated, crafty and ambitious woman with dreams of possessing a fortune of billions do if she ends up marrying a small-time thug with no identity of his own?

Answer: She uses her skills to shape her husband into a hardened gangster who ends up breathing fear into the moneyed class of the very city where he first began as a nobody, only a decade ago...

A middle-class Sikh by birth, Padma Poojary, nee Khanna, first met Ravi when she was studying at a co-educational convent school in the Mumbai suburb of Andheri. Both Padma and Ravi went to the same school in the Sahar Airport Colony.

Ravi, originally from Mangalore in Karnataka, soon

dropped out of school. From the very beginning, he was drawn to the world of crime and the underworld. After initially working as a small-time criminal, he rose through the ranks of the underworld when he killed his opponent Bala Zalte. Later, in the mid '90s, he went on to join self- proclaimed patriotic don Chhota Rajan's gang. Rajan, Dawood Ibrahim's aide-turned-enemy, was at the time trying to establish a strong base in Mumbai's crime scene. It was around this time that Ravi got married to his long-time girlfriend and childhood sweetheart Padma.

Padma only learned about Ravi's criminal activity after marrying him. She had two options: either to leave him or live with the fact that her husband was a goon. Lured by the possibility of immense wealth, she chose the latter, not really understanding, perhaps, the pitfalls of being married to a criminal.

Ravi served as Rajan's foot-soldier in Mumbai, starting off with executing the don's day-to-day orders. At Rajan's behest, he would extort money from hoteliers and other businessmen in Mumbai. In the years that followed, Poojary became one of Rajan's favourite protégés, travelling to Dubai and Southeast Asia to carry out his boss' jobs. Padma kept a low profile and continued to live with their children in a rented flat in the Sher-e-Punjab colony of Andheri in Mumbai.

Though Padma supposedly handled Ravi's extortion money while he was away, the police, for a long time, was oblivious to this 'housewife-cum-banker'. Perhaps the fact that she lived in a rented flat in the unremarkable and non-descript suburb of Andheri is one reason why the police didn't consider that she might be involved in his business.

During this time, Padma converted from Sikhism to Christianity and had her children baptised. The reason for this change of faith is still unknown.

By early 2000, Ravi had become one of Rajan's closest aides. However, barring the fact that he belonged to Rajan's gang, he did not have any extraordinary achievements or credentials that he could call his own. For a man who had always wanted to carve a niche for himself in the underworld, the realisation that he was a mere cog in the Rajan machinery was very disturbing.

According to police sources, it was during this time that Padma advised Ravi to deviate from the Rajan gang and start his own enterprise. She also allegedly suggested that he look at Bollywood and the business classes—the real mine of wealth. Following his wife's advice, Ravi left the Rajan gang and recruited men from Mumbai to work for him, even as he continued to operate from Southeast Asia. Extortion calls began to be made to bigwigs in the city. In 2006, Poojary's men opened fire at Bollywood director Mahesh Bhatt's office, after he refused to give in to Ravi's extortion demands. Poojary also tried to extort Rs 50 crore from Bollywood actress Karisma Kapoor's Delhi-based businessman husband Sanjay Kapur.

Padma shrewdly kept away from the gang's activities and escaped police scrutiny with consummate ease. Padma finally had her first brush with the law for obtaining a passport on the basis of a forged ration-card and school-leaving certificate in 1995. The matter concerning the submission of fake documents by Padma only came to light as late as 2005, a good ten years later, when she sent her passport for renewal and applied for her children's passports. The passport authorities grew suspicious while scrutinising her passport forms and immediately tipped off the Mumbai police's Crime Branch. The Crime Branch, on conducting inquires, learned that not only were the documents submitted for Padma's children's passport applications fake, but those submitted by her to procure a passport in 1995 had also been forged.

Padma had used the passport to travel to several countries in Africa and the Middle East. The police suspected that, during her course of travel, she had met her absconding husband, who had taken refuge in a foreign country. Her passport was seized and she was arrested on 4 October 2005. Padma was only released on bail some thirty days later. Her lawyer Shyam Keswani repeatedly denied her role in handling her husband's financial affairs. 'There is no truth in the police's claims,' he insisted. The police, too, did not have any evidence to book her for assisting Ravi in his activities.

However, following her arrest and bail, she came under police scrutiny. With her phone lines tapped and her whereabouts monitored by the police, Padma was left with no option but to flee the country. According to the police,

Padma escaped from India via the Nepal border after acquiring a new fake passport. The police only managed to arrest the person who planned her escape.

The Maharashtra police had issued an Interpol Red Corner Notice against Padma. The International Criminal Police Organisation, or Interpol as it is commonly known, spans 186 countries and assists national police in apprehending criminals. A Red Corner Notice is an indicator (in the form of a red flag) that pops up on the attendant's monitor if the person tries to check in at an airport, informing the attendant that this person is wanted. However, despite Interpol's backing, the police could not track Padma down and even five years after her escape, her location remains a mystery. The police believes that she is living with her husband and has narrowed down the location of her hideout to somewhere in South Africa.

Though Padma's criminal record is relatively less riddled with criminal activities as compared with Sujata Nikhalje, the wife of Chhota Rajan, she is the only wife of a Hindu gangster to have been portrayed on celluloid. A B-grade Bollywood film called *World Cupp 2011*, which released in early 2010, portrayed Padma Poojary as a hardcore drinker and the queen of cricket betting rackets, who bribed police authorities and government officials. The director of the film was later threatened by Ravi for portraying his wife in a negative light.

Padma's story cannot quite carry a 'The End' card, since it's impossible to predict the kind of designs Padma has drawn up for the future as chief architect of Ravi's gang's criminal activities.

Question: Where can an educated, crafty and ambitious woman with dreams of possessing a fortune of billions go if she ends up marrying a small-time thug with no identity of his own?

Answer: Anywhere she wants.

As far as the police is concerned, the chase is still on.

SEVEN

THE GANGLORD'S GIRLS

INTRODUCTION

A moll is often inadequately described as a 'gangster's girl'. For the average Indian who has grown up on a diet of Bollywood action potboilers, the first image the word 'moll' conjures up is that of a fair-skinned, scantily- clad woman blessed with a perfect physique with a penchant for imported liquor and cigarettes. She sways in nightclubs with the same grace and élan with which she sashays through the hearts of men. Her gambling habits at ritzy casinos are the stuff of legend, while she plays mischief-maker on demand at the insistence of her gangster boss.

However, reel life, as it does with most occupations, only serves to exaggerate the real. The gangster's girl in Mumbai's underworld is nothing like her depiction in cinema. She is, in fact, more brains than beauty, and certainly doesn't dance in clubs or sip on liquor all day.

The most prominent examples of molls in Mumbai's underworld are the tech-savvy Mrs Paul and the rotund beautician Rubina Siraj Sayyed, who were wooed by Dawood Ibrahim's Man Friday Chhota Shakeel. While Dawood's weakness is Bollywood bombshells, Shakeel's choices have been rather different—ordinary, even unattractive. But behind his choices lay an agenda. With most of his aides behind bars, Karachi-based Shakeel needed women who were less prone to scrutiny, to supervise the activities of his gang in Mumbai. And so he roped in the ambitious wives and female relatives of his most trusted aides to work for him. They took instructions from him on the phone or over the internet and carried out all tasks as spelled out to them.

However, Shakeel, who was normally a hard taskmaster, believed in sugar-coated conversations to motivate his women to work better. More often than not, these telephone sessions strayed into mushy, flirtatious repartee. It is this charisma that won Shakeel resourceful aides in women who, after being hypnotised by his flirtatious ways, often channelised all their energies to become efficient coordinators of the gang. Mrs Paul and Rubina belonged to this league.

MRS PAUL

If one were to rely solely on stereotypes, the name 'Mrs Paul' is most likely to evoke the image of a sixty-something Catholic woman with a polite demeanour. Dressed, possibly, in floral print summer dresses in pastel shades, she'd be the one narrating tales of her village somewhere in Goa to children, shopkeepers and fisherwomen alike. The only time this woman would be known to lose her temper would be when the fisherwoman overcharged her for her favourite tiger prawns.

If the police, intelligence agencies and informants used codenames for the purpose of furthering investigations, Mumbai's mafiosi, by coming up with misleading codenames, used them to throw a spanner or two in the police's works. One such red herring was Chhota Shakeel's business-cum-love interest, code-named 'Mrs Paul'. This particular Mrs Paul was in fact a twenty-eight-year-old tech-savvy, short and fair Muslim woman whose real name was Shameem Mirza Beg. She was the wife of Shakeel's most loyal lieutenant, Arif Beg.

Arif was doing time in the Kolhapur jail for his involvement in half-a-dozen killings, aiding in the escape of assassin Feroz Konkani in 1998 and single-handedly triggering the second round of communal riots in 1992-93 in Mumbai. He had introduced his wife to Shakeel much before his arrest, and had promised the don her full support in his absence. A little after Arif's arrest, Shameem started working for Shakeel under her uniquely deceptive code- name, Mrs Paul. The rationale behind giving her a Christian name was to send the police on a wild goose chase in search of a Christian woman, thereby keeping Shameem out of harm's way.

In next to no time, the Net-savvy, undergraduate woman was spending quality time with Shakeel on the phone and internet chat rooms.

The Crime Branch was tipped off about Mrs Paul in 2001. Phone lines were immediately tapped and their email ids hacked. Although it was some time before the police managed to work out who this Mrs Paul was, the virtual love affair that was carrying on between her and the don was soon exposed. For over a year the police tracked the conversations, in which Karachi-based Shakeel wooed Mumbai-based Mrs Paul, both sharing filmy-style love notes and photographs over the internet (Shakeel from handsomelovely@hotmail.com and Shameem from shams143@yahoo.com).

Excerpts from the 11 October 2001 conversation:

Shakeel: *Jaaneman, woh Nashik mein kapde aur saaman ki list* email *kar di hai.* (Darling, I have emailed the list of clothes and items needed in Nashik.)

Shameem: Cyber café *mein jaakar dekh loongi.* (I will go and have a look at a cyber café.)

(After some more business talk, the conversation turns romantic)

Shakeel: *Jaaneman, mujhe tumhari bahut yaad aa rahi hain, tumhare aane ka intezaar hain.* (Darling, I think of you a lot these days, I am waiting for you to come here.)

Shameem: *Jaan, main bhi aapko bahut yaad karti hoon.* (Darling, even I miss you a lot.)

Shakeel: I love you.

Shameem: I love you, too.

Through these conversations, the Mumbai police realised that Mrs Paul used three different cell phone numbers to communicate with Shakeel. The recordings exposed her role in Shakeel's business: she sent him hawala money, coordinated with his lawyers, and took care of the needs of his men lodged in various jails across the country. The phone recordings also revealed that Mrs Paul managed and supervised all of Chhota Shakeel's activities in Mumbai.

Mrs Paul was arrested in March 2002 under the Maharashtra Control of Organised Crime Act (MCOCA) and chargesheeted three months later. The chargesheet, comprising excerpts of the couple's phone conversations, read more like lines from a modern-day *Romeo and Juliet* or *Laila-Majnu*.

Most of the conversations were carried out in the kind of whispers and muffled voices that are usually used by teenage lovers desperate to keep their love a secret from others. According to the police, she would usually speak to Shakeel from inside the bathroom of her house until late at night, to avoid confrontation with her in-laws, with whom she lived.

Even though their relationship was so unusual—the two didn't meet each other at all during this time—issues of jealousy and complaints about distance, as seen in other relationships, ate into theirs too. For instance, in a phone conversation between the two on 8 January 2002, the Crime Branch learnt that Shakeel's wife had just delivered a son, something that upset Mrs Paul.

Excerpts from the 8 January 2002 conversation:

Shakeel: *Jaaneman tabiyat kaisi hai?* (Darling, how are you?)

Shameem: *Meri chhodiye, aapka baccha kaisa hain?*

(Forget about me, how is your son?)

Shakeel: *Bahut mannato ke baad paida hua hai, uski fikar toh karni padegi.* (He was born after a lot of prayers. I have to be bothered about him.)

Shameem: *Uski fikar main aap meri fikar chhod denge?* (Does this mean that you will forget about me?)

Shakeel: *Nahin jaaneman, uski jagah aur hai aur tumhari aur.* (No darling, both you and he hold different positions in my life.)

The cyber-savvy police also hacked into both Shameem and Shakeel's email accounts. Here, they found more love notes. In an email dated 12 March 2002, just before Shameem's arrest, Shakeel wrote her some lines picked up from a Bollywood film song.

Excerpts from the email:

Tujhko sunne ko dil chahta hain/ Tujhko milne ko dil chahta hain/ Teri jo ek jhalak aa jaaye nazar/ Tujh par marjaaoon yeh dil chaahta hain. (My heart wishes to listen to your voice / My heart wishes to meet you / I wish to get a glimpse of you / My heart wishes to die for you.)

> *Yaad tum bahut aati hon/ Taklif ka lamha hain/ Tumhaari awaaz sunne ko dil chahta hain.* (I think of you a lot / It is a very painful period for me / My heart wishes to listen to your voice.)

The police surmised that Shakeel must have written this letter when Shameem had failed to establish contact with him for a long period.

Ironically, when the police hacked into Shameem's email account, they learnt that this average-looking woman was extremely fickle in love. If being the wife of a gangster and girlfriend to a don wasn't enough, Shameem also engaged in other romantic liaisons. According to the police, she had a bunch of admirers, including a Parvez Batki who wrote to her from pbatki@hotmail.com. Initially the police suspected that it was Shakeel using a different ID, because the sender signed off as '*tumhara paagal premi*' (your mad lover), but Shameem averred that he was not Shakeel but one of her many admirers.

While the process of decoding an identity over time is usually nerve-wracking, in Mrs Paul's case, every subsequent conversation with Shakeel left the police more amused than confused.

RUBINA SIRAJ SAYYED

The Pathan hurled a plate of food at the face of the woman in front of her and bellowed, 'I don't want to eat this rice full of stones, roti made of hay and daal with insects in it!'

Livid, the woman—whose hands and face were covered with rice and watery daal—growled back, 'Pathan, you are not living in a palace. This is a jail and we only serve this kind of food here. Eat it, or else go to sleep.'

After the heated exchange, there was a moment of silence. They glared at each other, neither willing to be the first to look away or even blink. Then the jailer, who by now was accustomed to such brashness, tried to regain her lost composure and walked away to clean herself up. The Pathan, annoyed at how the jailer had dismissed the complaint, stormed out of the pantry area, hurling abuse and threatening the jailer with a court notice.

The Pathan being referred to in this confrontation was in fact not the tall, burly man one might have expected from the name, but a huge, uncouth, brusque woman in her late thirties. She had earned this sobriquet by virtue of being oversized and stocky. Intriguingly, despite her appearance, she was also addressed as 'heroine' by her fellow jail mates.

A city tabloid had first exposed her as 'Chhota Shakeel ki moti girlfriend' (Chhota Shakeel's fat girlfriend). It is this relationship with the underworld don that had pulled her from the comforts of her beauty parlour in south Mumbai into the Byculla Women's Jail. This is the story of Rubina Siraj Sayyed, a renowned beautician, who went on to become a renowned underworld aide.

First picked up by the Mumbai police in 2004, Rubina was convicted exactly two years later under the MCOCA for conspiracy charges. Her story is one of an ambitious woman who wanted to propel herself into the world of politics via the launch pad of the underworld.

A couple of years before her arrest, Rubina worked as a beautician in south Mumbai's Dongri area. Much in demand, she was called for several social events and weddings for her expensive beauty treatments. Although her annual income was high, far more than that of her civil contractor husband Siraj Sayyed, Rubina was not satisfied. She had bigger dreams. This mother of two wanted to join politics and become a municipal corporator. It was this drive that later drew her to the underworld.

It all began in 2002 when Rubina's brother-in-law Obaid Sayyed, a Shakeel aide, was arrested in a murder case and lodged in the Arthur Road Jail. During her occasional visits to the court and jail, Rubina was asked by Obaid to convey messages to Shakeel for him. She agreed. A smooth talker with a flirtatious voice, Rubina managed to flatter fugitive gangster Shakeel.

An impressed Shakeel then asked her to join the gang, an offer which was simply too lucrative for her to refuse. She assumed that her role in the underworld would boost her chances of contesting the municipal elections and becoming a municipal corporator. Hence, she started working for the gang almost immediately and carried out all the tasks she was given. She took instructions from Shakeel aide Fahim Mach-Mach, coordinated with lawyers, handled the financial affairs of all the gang members between south

Mumbai and Jogeshwari, and looked after all the needs of Shakeel's gangsters in jail. In only a few months, Rubina's lifestyle changed tremendously. Now more affluent than she had ever been, she moved from riding a two- wheeler to driving a car; and from being a beautician, she was now the notorious, powerful 'heroine' of an underworld gang.

Rubina was fluent in English and tech-savvy as well, which is why she managed to evade the police's electronic surveillance time and again. The Crime Branch only discovered her activities a year later, after one of Shakeel's men, Uday Pawar alias Pankaj, got in touch with her.

For a couple of a years, Pankaj had been demanding Rs 50 lakh from a film distributor and issuing threats to him. When the distributor agreed to pay Rs 10 lakh, Pankaj called Rubina to report this to her. The police happened to be listening in on this conversation. They soon began tracking Rubina's movements and calls, and in the process, recorded twenty-six conversations made to Fahim Mach-Mach and Shakeel. After watching her movements closely for over four months, the Crime Branch finally arrested her in 2004.

According to the police, at the last count, she was looking after twenty-five families of men affiliated to the Shakeel gang and would distribute Rs 1.5 lakh among them every month, apart from making payments for legal expenses. The special MCOCA court convicted her for charges under MCOCA and 120 (b) (Conspiracy) of the IPC and sentenced her to five years of rigorous imprisonment on 23 March 2006. Her case was fought by advocate Shahid Azmi, who years later, in February 2010, fell victim to a former shooter of the Chhota Rajan gang.

Rubina's conceit and arrogance only seemed to increase during her years in jail. The jail authorities were regularly inundated with complaints from prison inmates against Rubina for assaulting them. Among the most prominent of these cases was when Rubina, along with her cellmate and Gateway blast-accused Fahmida Sayyed, had attacked a diminutive Zahira Sheikh, who was serving out her perjury sentence in the Gujarat Best Bakery case. Following this, jail authorities punished Rubina by barring her from buying jail canteen coupons, which otherwise provided inmates access to luxury goods, such as soaps, biscuits, toothpaste and dry fruit.

Today, after completing her five-year term in jail, Rubina is a free woman, but her time behind bars has sent her back to square one. Rubina, who lost her husband Siraj recently, is back to riding a two-wheeler and has nothing that she can consider to be a source of livelihood. While her parlour business shut down years ago, her political dreams, too, have not been realised. The once well-known beautician and Shakeel aide is far from being the underworld's favourite Pathani heroine anymore, she'd be hard-pressed to even be deemed an extra.

EIGHT

BEWITCHING BEAUTIES

INTRODUCTION

It is not only Bollywood actresses and supermodels who rake in millions of rupees with their ravishing looks. Sometimes, they are also Ram Leela artistes and bar dancers, whose looks and powers of manipulation are worthy allies in helping them make their fortunes. These women don't enjoy the privilege of being the wives of dons; neither do they take pride in being arm candy for their bosses in the underworld. But with the innate gift to turn a hundred heads, these seductive women have trapped several men in their nets as they lied, cheated, deceived, conned and masterminded sensational crimes. While there are many who fit the bill, we narrowed it down to two exceptionally notorious women who used their personality and charismatic looks as weapons for crime.

'Crorepati bar girl' Tarannum Khan was arguably one of the richest and most controversial faces of Mumbai's nightlife. Tarannum was in the news for weeks due to her alleged involvement in an international cricket betting racket. The stunning bar dancer made crores by betting on the sport; apparently it was at her house that the ill-gotten money of an international cricketer was stashed. The scandal brought to light the sharp brain behind an otherwise innocent face. While Tarannum is not part of the hardcore mafia, her role in the global betting syndicate makes her story a sensational one.

The second woman, Archana Sharma, was willing to go to any extent to make a quick buck. Labelled by a prominent tabloid as the 'lady don with killer looks', Archana used her sex appeal to entrap businessmen, politicians and hoteliers. She had no qualms about simultaneously bed-hopping with politicos and gangsters to win favours and realise her dreams. Slapped with several cases of kidnappings, murders and extortion, this small-town girl from Ujjain epitomises daredevilry and fearlessness.

TARANNUM KHAN

At a time when most of Mumbai goes to sleep, the dance bars wake up. At two in the morning, one such suburban Mumbai bar is bursting with the energy of blaring music, debauched men, vivacious girls and free-flowing alcohol. The air is pregnant with the lust for sex and money. The place is crammed beyond capacity but the mirrored walls create the illusion of space.

Men throng here in large numbers to enjoy a break from their monotonous existences for a few hours of fantasy. They drink away their worries and smoke like chimneys. However, even in their semi-conscious alcoholic daze, their bodies warm to the presence of a few girls on the dance floor in the centre. The girls are dressed skimpily in shimmering lehenga cholis and are gyrating to loud Bollywood music that jars as it emanates from the speakers. Heavily made-up, these girls share a faint resemblance to big-screen starlets. All eyes are on them as they dance like slaves for their patrons. These patrons aren't ordinary, though; among them, you will find money-laden businessmen, diamond merchants, gangsters, industrialists and celebrities who are willing to spend their fortunes in return for a few moments of visual gratification.

Some of the dancers have already chosen their prey from among these filthy-rich admirers and make eye-contact and gestures in their direction while sashaying across the dance floor. Their movements become bolder with every song. In return, their admirers approach them with garlands of 100-rupee notes. The girls lean forward but remain within the confines of the floor. As they are garlanded, their soft silky hair brushes the skin of their patrons, who then express their approval by showering them with money. But while a few have already chosen the woman of their fantasies, others are still grudgingly holding onto their bundles of notes. In Mumbai lingo, the 'big maal' is yet to come.

Half-an-hour later, the music suddenly veers to the popular Bollywood track—*Kajra Re*. The lights grow dimmer and all of a sudden a girl, draped in a glittering translucent pink sari with a cleavage-revealing blouse, cavorts onto the floor. Just like the Pied Piper, she manages to draw the attention of each and every one towards her. The other girls suddenly seem like extras in comparison.

There is a roar in the crowd when she raises her arms and moves her hips first to the right, then the left, before she begins to dance. When the beat of the song quickens, she has her admirers in a trance. She rotates her shoulders in a small circular motion and waves her hands, while heaving her breasts forwards. She also lip-syncs the words of the song with suggestive expressions and spares no one with her lascivious winks. There is nothing extraordinary about her. She has long black hair, pale wheatish skin and is only as pretty as the other girls, yet no one can take their eyes off her. In no time, 500 and 1,000-rupee notes begin to fly like a deck of cards in her direction. The other bar girls continue swaying on the sidelines, envious of her for grabbing all the attention. Like her melodic name, she has captivated everyone with her tune.

Tarannum Khan was the pin-up girl of suburban Mumbai's Deepa Bar and Restaurant. At the age of twenty-four, Tarannum was no less popular than any Bollywood starlet. A high-profile bar girl, she allegedly made over Rs 1.5 to Rs 3 lakh every day, and attracted a clientele that comprised the affluent and the famous. She was the crown of Mumbai's nightlife until she was arrested for her links to an international cricket betting racket.

An Income Tax department raid in 2005 at her

bungalow—Tanishq—in suburban Mumbai, unearthed pieces of a puzzle that could not only land her in trouble, but also jeopardise the careers of some of the world's most celebrated sportsmen. Her miseries began to unfold like a nightmare as she made the headlines almost every day.

However, the tale of one of Mumbai's most controversial bar girls actually had its beginnings in the struggles and hardships she underwent as a teenager. Although she had a diploma in computer education, Tarannum's ambitions lay elsewhere—she wanted to become an air-hostess.

However, times were rough for Tarannum's family. Her parents had already endured grave financial loss when their home at Sion in central Mumbai was set on fire during the Hindu-Muslims riots of 1992-93. Further, Tarannum's mother, who suffered from diabetes and a heart problem, needed immediate medical attention. And so at the young age of seventeen, Tarannum had to give up on her dreams and do menial jobs to meet the medical expenses of her ailing mother. Her efforts were either too little or simply inadequate. This is when she took to dancing at bars.

Tarannum's popularity soared to such heights that within a year, she was called to Dubai to perform for a few clients. She was unremittingly showered with money and gifts. It wasn't long before she could buy herself a plot from the MHADA—a state body that provides affordable housing—in the posh locality of Versova in Mumbai, where she later built a bungalow.

Tarannum flourished as a bar dancer. She captivated

and wooed rich businessmen and film stars alike, and saw no reason to look for greener pastures—until 2005. Ironically, this was the same year that marked the death-knell for all dance bars in Mumbai. The then home minister of Maharashtra R.R. Patil called for a ban on dance bars across the state. Citing it as detrimental to society, the minister set an early deadline of August 15 for dance bar owners to shut shop. Even before Mr Patil could seal the fate of the bars, several dancers began looking for alternative sources of livelihood. While most looked for lucrative options in the neighbouring states of Goa, Andhra Pradesh and Karnataka, others turned to prostitution.

However, Deepa Bar's Tarannum, who had been entertaining clients for over seven years and was used to making big money, saw the potential in cricket betting. Her clientele had included some avid cricket bookies and with their help, she started taking serious bets on the game and her earnings tripled in no time.

On 29 August 2005, Income Tax officials raided Tarannum's bungalow when they learnt that she had failed to file her I-T returns for over four years. Incidentally, the MHADA had also been planning to issue a notice against her for not complying with property tax rules. During the raid, I-T officials seized over Rs 22 lakh in cash, and gold jewellery worth Rs 8 lakh from her bungalow that was now worth Rs 1.25 crore. In her defence, Tarannum claimed that she had not filed her I-T returns because her chartered accountant had misguided her.

Her troubles were not to end here. Further investigations by I-T officials shockingly revealed the phone numbers of some notorious cricket bookies and an international Sri Lankan cricketer on her cell phone. The case was immediately handed over to the Mumbai police to probe if Tarannum was in any way associated with a betting racket.

Several names emerged during the investigations, including bookie-turned producer Jagdish Sodha, bookies Shobhan Mehta, Pradip Kumar and Milind Dhiraj Nandu, alias DJ. The police had also found enough evidence to show that she had placed bets for an Australia-England match on 20 August 2005, for which she was to receive anywhere between Rs 20 to 30 lakh.

However, the case took a sensational turn when the names of Bollywood actor Aditya Panscholi and Sri Lankan spinner Muttiah Muralitharan surfaced during the investigations. There were reports that the actor had taken Muttiah, who was in Mumbai for a cricket match, to the bar and introduced him to Tarannum. There were rumours that Tarannum apparently stashed the spinner's illegal money, earned through betting, in her home. While both Aditya and Muttiah did not deny having visited the bar, they vehemently refuted the charges of being associated with Tarannum or of being involved in match-fixing. The police eventually cleared their names. Meanwhile, contradictory stories about Tarannum's notorious past, which included her alleged links with the underworld and her involvement in the flesh trade, also came to the fore.

In an interview, Tarannum, who until then was elusive and unapproachable to the media, denied any involvement with cricketers. Excerpts from the interview:*

> While Tarannum was entirely unapologetic about her involvement in cricket betting, she openly denied that she knew any cricketers. 'I bet, but don't know cricketers,' she said.
>
> With a straight face, she said that her involvement in cricket betting went back 'only six months' and claimed that the Rs 22 lakh seized by the I-T department from her Versova bungalow was her own and not that of any cricketer's. She also admitted to knowing bookie-turned film producer Jagdish Sodha, who along with another bookie Shobhan Mehta, allegedly passed on the cricketer's money to her. Sodha has also been accused by the Mumbai police of paying Rs 8 lakh to the cricketer in September 2004 to fix matches in the ICC Knockout tournament, which was played in England.
>
> 'I know Sodha very well, though I don't know Shobhan Mehta. I started betting on cricket six months ago and have wagered with just one bookie, called DJ. I have been betting anything between Rs 15,000 and Rs 25,000,' she said in fluent English.

* Published in the *Mumbai Mirror*, 15 September 2005

She noted that she had always harboured the impression that punters did not commit any crime by betting on the game. 'It is only the bookies who violate the law,' she said.

The dancer claimed the bungalow on SVP Road, Versova, where she lived, was bought with her 'hard- earned' money. 'I bought the bungalow for Rs 27 lakh from the MHADA five years ago, when the land here was marshy and deserted. You can check the MHADA records. Why would bookies and cricketers gift this to me? The cash, too, is my money, which I saved over a period of seven to eight years. It does not belong to any bookie or some ugly- looking cricketer,' she said, brashly.

When asked how she could accumulate so much money if she worked as a bar girl, she said, 'I had an affluent clientele. All my patrons worked with multinationals. Any bar girl can do thumkas, but regular visitors knew me for my original dances and rewarded me for my talent, not for my looks.'

She also denied links with the underworld. 'The Crime Branch is well aware that I don't know anyone in the underworld.' She also asserted that she never indulged in prostitution. 'Prostitution is a matter of choice; a girl can say no. Only girls in those bars which are downmarket and have patrons like truck drivers may have to resort to prostitution.

> Upmarket bars don't get involved in such practices,' she said. She expressed the hope that dance bars would reopen so she could get back to her work. What if they don't? 'If I had this money which has been seized, I would have started some business,' she said.

Tarannum subsequently gave television interviews but chose to appear veiled in her burqa. The grapevine was full of rumours about what the real Tarannum looked like. Some local newspapers published photographs of a woman claiming that she was the real bar girl. Later, Telugu film starlet Tamanna Bhatia filed a complaint against several newspapers and demanded action against them for carrying her photo and labelling it as Tarannum's.

Finally, on 15 September 2005, the police, under intense pressure from the state government and the media, arrested Tarannum, along with two other bookies, under the charges of criminal conspiracy and gambling. For the first time, the police invoked provisions of the Information Technology (IT) Act in a gambling case and slapped charges of misuse of IT against the trio. Tarannum had to spend the next two months at the Byculla Women's Jail before she was granted bail by a sessions court in November 2005.

After receiving bail, a disturbed Tarannum complained about how she was being treated. 'Now, people point at my home and say, "Look, this is the house where the bar girl stays". Now all of India knows about me. I want an answer from the government: what will happen if all the allegations levelled against me are false? Who will be responsible for it?' she had said in an interview.

Apparently, while behind bars, Tarannum had bonded well with actress Preeti Jain, who was her cellmate. Preeti, who had stirred a hornet's nest after she had alleged that Bollywood director Madhur Bhandarkar had raped her, was also serving time in the same jail. She had been charged for allegedly hiring gangster Arun Gawli's hitman to kill the director. The actress spent around thirteen days with the bar girl in the same cell, before she was bailed out. Months after her release, she signed a lead role in the low-budget film titled *Deepa ki Tarannum,* a movie on a bar dancer, which in Preeti's words was inspired by 'her friend in jail'.

Reminiscing about her days with the bar girl, Preeti told us that Tarannum had spent most of her time in the jail crying. According to Preeti, Tarannum was initially traumatised and frightened at the thought of being locked behind bars and would break down often. 'As a human being, I could relate to her pain. I became a shoulder for her to cry on,' Preeti said.

Later, the duo bonded really well and became comfortable in each other's company. As Preeti said, 'During those few days I spent with her, we played board games, ate food and also watched television together.' The starlet maintained that Tarannum was no run-of-the-mill bar dancer. She claimed that Tarannum was extremely beautiful and not only well-groomed but well-spoken. 'People have this preconceived notion about bar girls being crass. Tarannum was anything but that. The best part is that she did not regret being a bar dancer or care about the stigma that the job brought with it.'

In March 2008, Tarannum was again in the news after she approached the I-T department and demanded all the money it had seized. However, both troubled and discomfited from being under the constant media glare, she left Mumbai for good and gradually faded into obscurity. Her current whereabouts are not known, but according to sources, she has relocated to Dubai and is supposedly catering to the rich and elite there.

As for Deepa Bar and Restaurant, the absence of its star performer and the ban on dance bars changed its fortunes forever. One of the most notorious night hubs in its heyday, the 4,500-square feet property is now being converted into a haven of spirituality, with a yoga and medical centre being planned there.

ARCHANA SHARMA ALIAS MANISHA

Her face was the epitome of innocence; her tears broke a hundred hearts and her performances moved a million. She was the face of Ujjain's annual Ram Leela performance as the goddess Sita. However, no one knew when their Sita decided to swap roles with one of the *Ramayan's* most demonic characters and decided to play Ravan in real life.

Archana Balmukund Sharma took the underworld by storm as she executed several sensational murders, kidnappings and extortions, to become one of India's most wanted female gangsters. Considered a close confidante of gangster Babloo Srivastav and branded the 'lady don with killer looks' by the *Pune Mirror*, Archana used her sex appeal and resemblance to Bollywood actress Manisha Koirala to entrap businessmen and hoteliers alike. Hers is the story of the transformation of a well-educated innocent girl from Madhya Pradesh into a hard-boiled criminal, who was willing to go the extra mile to make a quick buck and enjoy a lavish lifestyle.

The eldest of four children, Archana was born in the town of Ujjain in Madhya Pradesh on 17 November 1975. She belonged to a lower-middle class family but her father Balmukund Sharma, a former platoon commander of the Home Guard, made certain she received a good education. As a young girl, Archana was known to be affable, talented and creative. She spent most of her time painting and participating in cultural activities in Ujjain, and never missed the annual Ram Leela that was conducted by Mouni Baba (the eminent saint of Malwa).

After finishing her higher secondary education from Central School, Archana joined the BA course at Vikram University in Ujjain. She dropped out after her first year however, and was recruited by the state police. The news of her recruitment into the police force brought great pride to the family but the excitement did not last long. Six months later, much to her family's disappointment, she quit the job because of the rigorous working hours. She then left home and moved to Bhopal, in search of a more exciting life.

In Bhopal, Archana was employed by Som Distilleries Private Ltd as a receptionist. While working there, she befriended several Congress and Bharatiya Janata Party MLAs and was also accused of having a brief affair with a BJP MLA. Archana used this exposure to perfect her manners and polish her language skills.

Right from her Ram Leela days, Archana had harboured the desire to become a Bollywood actress. This aspiration finally brought her to Mumbai—the heart of Bollywood—in the early 1990s. She used the pseudonym Manisha Agarwal and tried to sell herself as the lookalike of actress Manisha Koirala. But in Bollywood, where clones don't find success easily, Archana ended up sharing the same fate of many other strugglers like her.

Her brief flings with small-time actors and directors also failed to help her get film roles. Disillusioned and disappointed, Archana took all the odd jobs she got in the film and television industry. She eventually ended up in an orchestra that performed in the Gulf. Though the job paid her well, it did not give her the lifestyle she desired.

Then in 1994, Archana got her first prize catch. She was in Dubai as part of pop singer Baba Sehgal's troupe, when she met businessman Pritam Miglani from Ahmedabad. Archana managed to woo Pritam, who succumbed to her wiles and helped her get a resident's visa in Dubai. He also assisted her in opening a garment store in Sharjah. The couple got engaged in Ujjain and decided to get married in Dubai.

But the wedding never took place as the couple parted ways acrimoniously. Archana shifted to Mumbai once again and re-established ties with her family. However, after failed attempts to get good work, she returned to Dubai. Her destiny was shaped by that very move.

During her stay in Dubai, her path crossed that of gangster Irfan Goga, a former Anees Ibrahim aide. Archana, who was instantly attracted to his opulent lifestyle, did not have any qualms about becoming his mistress. Goga, in turn, put her up in a flat and introduced her to several of his criminal friends, including Chhota Rajan's right hand Om Prakash, alias Babloo Srivastav.

Archana managed to charm her way into Babloo's heart and he decided to train her into becoming a perfect criminal. She did not disappoint him. Babloo was madly in love with her, while she needed him to further her own plans. Together, the couple made a lethal combination. It is from here that her tumultuous journey in the world of crime took off.

After a few months in Dubai, the couple fled to Nepal where Babloo was soon arrested and deported to India. Archana followed her mentor to India, where he made arrangements for her to live in Sunlight Colony, New Delhi. She had wasted no time in becoming a vital cog in Babloo's business as she started executing orders ruthlessly, often luring unsuspecting kidnap victims with the charm that once failed to get her into showbiz.

Archana carried out her first independent operation in 1998, using the assumed name Salma. With the help of Babloo's gang, she masterminded the kidnapping of hotelier Lala Vyas and collected a huge ransom. The Delhi police, however, was tipped off about the plot and raided her apartment where they found and confiscated several automatic rifles. They were also able to get details of the gang's earlier operations, which included the kidnapping of another wealthy hotelier. Through Lala Vyas, the police also learnt that Archana was plotting the kidnapping of several businessmen in Delhi.

She was also wanted by the Mumbai police for the sensational kidnapping of builder R.D. Vyas—the only time that Archana actually involved herself in the execution of a plan. The operation had been carried out with the help of two others belonging to Babloo's gang but it was Archana who had contacted Vyas. She told him that his friend in Dubai had sent some goods for him and asked if he could meet her at a hotel. Once there, she used her acting prowess and good looks to persuade him that the goods were at her residence, and to accompany her there. Vyas literally walked into the trap and was only released after his family paid Rs 4 crore as ransom.

Archana was finally arrested, and later let out on bail, which she promptly jumped. The police arrested some of her gang members, but 'Madame X'—as the police referred to her—remained elusive.

In April 1998, four of her associates were killed in Indore after they had collected a ransom of Rs 30 lakh from a small-time trader, Jagdish Modi Ramani. Archana, who was in the city planning the operation, ran away and managed to evade arrest.

These close shaves did not deter Archana. She stopped visiting her family as the police was watching them. And, after the one time when she had been part of the execution of a plan, she never made that mistake again. Like her mentor Babloo, she just chose the target and planned the operation but never participated in the actual act. Her strategy helped in keeping her out of harm's way. In December 1998, Archana and her gang planned to kidnap another industrialist in Kolkata, but the Uttar Pradesh police got wind of it and tracked them to Park Street in Kolkata. Four gangsters were killed in the shootout, but Archana, who was at a nearby hotel, got away. Within minutes of the shootout, she was on board a plane to Nepal, where she stayed till the situation had calmed down. The police had missed its chance again.

Archana continued to come up with plots to kidnap other businessmen. She was also suspected to have been behind the attempted kidnapping of businessman Babubhai Singhvi in Kutch and the kidnapping of exporter Gautam Adani in Ahmedabad.

Archana was also notorious for how she used men to get what she wanted. While she was in a relationship with Babloo, she had a brief affair with kidnapper Fazal-ur-Rehman, alias Fazloo. She is said to have plotted the murder of Pune businessman and petrol pump owner Sagar Ladkat along with Fazal.

According to the police, Ladkat was returning to his house in Koregaon Park from his Somwar Peth petrol pump on the night of 22 May 1998, when members of the Fazal-ur-Rehman gang intercepted his car and whisked him away to Kondhwa. He was hacked to death there and his mutilated body was abandoned in his car. Investigations later revealed that Archana had masterminded the crime, although it remained unconfirmed why the victim was killed.

Even though Archana continued to have brief flings, she remained the jewel in Babloo's crown. The gangster was so possessive about her that he could not tolerate anyone else getting close to her. Former Nepal minister Mirza Dilshad Beg of the Rashtriya Prajatantra Party paid a huge price for his alleged closeness to Archana. After Babloo was deported from Nepal, Beg apparently became very close to Archana, which infuriated the gangster. Babloo suspected that the minister had not helped prevent his deportation as he wanted Archana all to himself. In June 1998, Beg was killed by Chhota Rajan gangsters while he was on his way home after visiting his wife in Kathmandu.

There was a rumour that Archana was shot dead in Nepal in May 2010, after she conned some drug traffickers. The *Pune Mirror*, however, reported that she was killed by rivals who were on her trail in Nepal, where she had been hiding for over two years. Still others claim that she is just lying low for the time being, perhaps plotting her next big crime.

ACKNOWLEDGEMENTS

Soon after we took up the task of writing this book, we realised that the world was full of generous and helpful people whose support made this project not only possible but so much more easier.

Our foremost thanks are reserved for my editor-in-chief, Ram Reddy, of the *Deccan Chronicle*. I am grateful to Ram for giving me the professional latitude to venture ahead in writing the book.

We owe the completion of this book to our colleague at *The Asian Age*, Karan Pradhan. We started this project in March last year but realised that it had barely moved forward even six months later. It was then that Karan, with his myriad talents, offered to help in the expeditious completion of the project. With his unmatchable understanding of editing, Karan gave some much-needed impetus to our crawling project. He became our sounding board, co-strategist, ideator, editor and also wore several more hats. In the end, if the stories looked good, it was because of his work. We would both like to express our heartfelt thanks to Karan. Thank you, Karan ... we are glad that you were associated with the book.

My editor at Westland, Deepthi Talwar, a young and bubbly girl, convinced me to pen a book on women criminals and did not relent until I was persuaded to compile one. She remained patient and painstakingly put up with my ways, to ensure that the book went to print.

While the book encapsulates the lives of only thirteen women, their stories have been narrated and fleshed out with the help of several others. We will always be indebted to them for helping us ensure the book saw the light of day. Jenabai's story mainly came from her eldest daughter, Khadija Darwesh, and an article from the renowned Urdu tabloid *Akbhaar-e-Alam*. While we'd like to thank Khadija for throwing some light on her mother, our sincere thanks also goes out to former chief reporter of the daily, *The Urdu Times,* Suhas Bhiwankar, veteran journalist Shakeel Rashid of *Urdu Times,* police historian Deepak Rao and Adil Bhesadia, for helping us align the sequence of events in Jenabai's life. We would also like to thank the *Indian Express* principal correspondent Anita Nair who provided us with vital information about Vardharajan, his devotion to the Muslim saint and his life through her journalistic sources and interviews with his family. The rest of the story was put together after interviewing her neighbours and other sources, who preferred not to be mentioned. We would also like to thank retired Crime Branch officers like Madhukar Zende and Ishaq Bagwan, who opened several doors of information for us.

Gangubai's account came from Suhas, who made us walk miles and miles in the red light district of south Mumbai, since he was just too restless to sit at one place and talk. But we must admit that Gangubai's story was worth the walk. Suhas provided interesting nuggets of information, which helped in building the narrative of our story. We would also like to thank senior inspector Shamsher Pathan of the Pydhonie police station. Pathan saab was of immense help, as he introduced us to several locals at Kamathipura. I must also thank my old contact Rafeeq Lala, who agreed to talk to me and give me vast information on Gangubai's close bond with the Pathan ganglord Karim Lala.

The most difficult story was that of Ashraf Khan, alias Sapna didi. Her daring tale came by me by accident, and for this, I must thank my friend and author of *Sacred Games,* Vikram Chandra. Vikram and I met gangster Hussain Sheikh, alias Ustara, as part of our research for Vikram's book. It is during this time that Ustara opened up and started talking about Sapna didi. Since I was taking down the notes, I managed to put her story together. Vikram later mentioned his brief encounter with Ustara in his article, titled 'The Cult of Authenticity', which was published in *The Boston Review*. Thank you, Vikram, for allowing me to use this interesting anecdote in my book.

Sapna didi's story was also authenticated by some Crime Branch officers and police officers from the Nagpada police station. We also got some insight on Ustara and

Sapna didi's relationship from Asif and Feroz (full names withheld at their request).

Our fourth story was about drug mafia queen Mahalaxmi Papamani. During my days of crime reporting at the *Indian Express* in 1997, I had written extensively about the Papamani menace. However, I must say that Jane Borges' work was a revelation to me. She diligently pieced Papamani's story together after meeting narcotics lawyer Ayaz Khan and several officers of the Narcotics Control Bureau and Anti-Narcotics Cell.

Our sincere thanks to all the senior officers of the NCB, and officers from Azad Maidan who wished to remain unnamed. We would also like to thank senior officer Dilip Shrirao, Girish Koende of the ANC, inspector Arun Kumar Aigal and Central Excise inspector Mallika Pattabhiraman for helping us source the right contacts.

Some of the information for our story came from drug peddlers. While it is not possible to name all of them, Jyoti Adiramlingam and her daughter Asha Yadav of Reay Road were our primary sources, in addition to the twenty-odd women who were rounded up the ANC and exclusively interviewed by Jane while they did time in the Azad Maidan lock-up.

But our heartfelt thanks are reserved for Ayaz Khan and *DNA* court correspondent Menaka Rao. We would also like to mention the contribution made by our friend Tess Joss and journalist friend Arundhati Pattabhiraman of *The Asian Age*. Both of them took risks and showed exemplary courage when they accompanied Jane on one of her several visits to Jyoti and Papamani's hide-outs.

The last of the five main chapters was on Monica Bedi. The treatment of Monica's story was tricky. It was difficult to compile the story of a reluctant subject like her. Despite repeated assurances that we would do justice to her story, Monica remained adamant and refused to talk to us. Fortunately, the Central Bureau of Investigation officers like deputy superintendent of police Raman Tyagi and Retd. DSP Devendra Pardesi, both of whom had worked on the case, came to our rescue. They helped us plug the loopholes in Monica's story by sharing with us previously unknown information.

However, we would especially like to thank Jigna Vora of *The Asian Age*. She gave us access to reams and reams of documents on Monica to ensure accuracy in our storytelling. Jigna also provided us with the romantic letters that Monica wrote to Salem while she was locked up in the Lisbon jail. Exercising our discretion, we only culled specific information and refrained from revealing anything that would make our narrative salacious or sensational. In the process, we also referred to interviews Monica had given to magazines like *Outlook, Showtime* and newspaper articles in *The Asian Age, Mid-Day, Times of India, Mumbai Mirror* and *PTI*. We also referred to videos from reality television show *Bigg Boss 2* that are now in the public domain. But the icing on the cake was the article by senior editor, Lakshmi Govindrajan, for the Heartitude column of *The*

Asian Age. The article was immensely helpful in ensuring that we did not falter in expressing Monica's emotions in our story. I would also like to thank my Spanish friend Professor Dora Sales. She helped us translate Portuguese work related to Monica's incarceration. Thank you Dora, for replying to our queries when we needed your inputs the most.

Our special thanks also go to starlet Preeti Jain who willingly opened up to us on Tarannum Khan for our chapter, 'Bewitching Beauties', and assistant police inspector Avinash Dharmadhikari for providing vital information on gangster Ravi Poojary's wife Padma.

We can never finish thanking all those who helped in contributing in their own special way; however, we need to thank some of our friends and co-workers in the media. The list is long but their names cannot go unmentioned. These include *Mumbai Mirror* resident editor Pankaj Upadhyay, *Mid-Day* editor Abhijit Majumdar, Suresh Karkera and Vinod Kumar Menon of *Mid-Day,* Neeraj Priyadarshi from the *Indian Express,* Mateen Hafeez of *Times of India,* senior crime reporter, the late Pradeep Shinde, and our colleagues at *The Asian Age,* Prasad Patil, Dippy Vankani, Mohammed Hassan Kamal, Anand Shinde and Amit Haralkar. Among other colleagues at *The Asian Age,* Aditya Prakash Iyengar undertook the arduous task of proofreading and went through each and every punctuation mark to save us from embarrassment.

I would like to make a special mention of my personal

assistant, the super efficient Pramodini Amin, who pitched in in her own way to help me complete the project.

We cannot overlook the immense moral support Saby and Steven provided to Jane, proving to her again that they are the best siblings in the world. Thank you very much my sweet bros, what will I do without you, says Jane.

We would also like to thank our friends, Mikhael Fidel D'Souza, Bonnie Vaz and Vinod Joe, who are not journalists but showed journalistic zeal and willingly tagged along with us whenever required.

I need to specially express my profound gratitude to my nutritionist, Shabana Husain, who was very proficient at her job. Shabana's elixir-filled recipes ensured that I was brimming with high octane energy all the time and my stress levels were kept in check.

My thanksgiving will not be complete until I express my gratitude to my favourite women, Fatema Zahra and Narjis Zahra, who make me look at the world with a youthful perspective.

And the apples of my eyes, Ammar and Zain, who with their loving hugs keep driving me to give my best to what I do.

My copious thanks to my beloved friend, *The Asian Age*'s news editor Megha Moorthy, who is my biggest detractor on the planet. She brainstormed with us, read and edited with me to ensure we created a story that was as compelling as it was readable.

I would like to add my sincere thanks to filmmaker

Vishal Bhardwaj who readily agreed to write a foreword for the book and delivered it on time, making time from his busy shooting schedule in Russia.

My most heartfelt thanks are reserved for my worst critic, teacher and my wife, Velly Thevar, who taught me how to think, believe and most importantly write. Velly kept my feet firmly planted on terra firma.

In the end, I would once again mention that one individual who made me believe in myself and encouraged me to become an author again, Vikram Chandra. Vikram told me in 1997 that I should write a book and last year he reiterated that I should write more often. Despite his work pressures, Vikram devoted immense attention to the book, read it several times, corrected the flaws, guided me with the correct format and suggested the title of the book. No amount of gratitude and kind words can be adequate in expressing thanks for his contribution to the current work. Shukriyaa, karam, meherbani, my friend Vikram Chandra.

We have made our best efforts to be absolutely accurate and truthful in our narrations. However, it is quite possible there may be some mistakes due to human error. We confess that while all the accuracies belong to the people mentioned above, the inaccuracies and flaws are all ours.